Chapter 1

• •

I have an incredible life," I exclaimed as I danced across the large bedroom of my apartment. By 1985, I'd reached the top of my profession. Although four years would pass before Joan Rivers dubbed me "Queen of the Jingles," my life was zooming forward. I had money, jewelry, furs, and all the work I wanted. I'd fulfilled every one of my childhood ambitions.

Well, almost every one.

For once in a while when I was alone my thoughts would return to my childhood in Detroit. I'd especially think of my grandfather and Aunt Helen. Sadness would come over me and I'd ask myself, *What am I doing with my life? I have so many things, but is that all there is? Shouldn't there be more in life?*

However, I could never figure out what I meant by "more." More accurately, I didn't want to know. Fortunately, those moments of introspection didn't come often. When they did, I'd bury them with shopping—my way to avoid facing the unpleasant parts of my life. But now and then I tried to imagine what my friends would say if I mentioned the emptiness I sometimes felt. They'd probably laugh and say, "You have a world of friends and so many clothes and jewels. What more could you want?" Or they might chide me and say, "Honey, you've got everything. Just enjoy it."

And I did enjoy the exciting lifestyle. Most of the time.

I didn't realize those occasional moments would become more frequent and the emptiness would get worse during the next few years. In 1985 I was too busy playing out the role of

Queen of the Jingles to think about what was missing. Producers knew my work, and asked for me by name. When I first moved to New York in 1975, I took the jobs that others didn't want. At the same time, friends such as Frank Floyd and Patti Austin opened doors for me. Then came my big break. I started working with Billy Davis, who composed jingles for Coca Cola and other giant corporations. He'd written a delightful jingle called, "I'd Like to Teach the World to Sing," and I had recorded the solo portion and had been part of the background vocals as well.

In 1983, the Coke people decided to put their old spots back on the air, including "I'd Like to Teach the World to Sing." In the new TV version, done primarily for the Christmas season, the camera panned a large group of students standing on a mountaintop. They sang, and although I didn't appear on the film Billy hired me to do the solo part. I was the voice behind the song.

Shortly afterward, Billy told me, "Coke is making a lot of changes in their products. It's still not public knowledge, but they're going to get rid of their old drink and bring in a new Coke." He gave me a big smile as he said that he'd been hired to do the music and he wanted me to sing the jingle.

"Great!" I cried. "I'm ready." I was absolutely elated. Coke spent a lot of money promoting their product and every time one of my commercials aired, they sent me a nice residual check.

"Coke is based in Atlanta," Billy said, "and they're setting up a big, big deal there." He told me they'd already hired Ray Charles to sing the Coke song. "It works like this. Ray starts to sing, and right in the middle, you walk on stage and join in singing with him. You two close the new spot together. That's all. Not a big thing, but—"

"Sounds wonderful to me," I said, thrilled to get the opportunity.

Coke would pay all my travel expenses, he explained, provide me with the costume they wanted me to wear, and then pay me a fee. "So, now that you know the deal, are you interested?"

"Are you kidding? I would love to do it."

Billy hesitated as though he had something to tell me and he didn't know if it would make me mad. "It's not much money," he began.

I didn't care. I was just happy to get the job.

"I had no right to speak up for you," he said, and I could tell he was embarrassed, "but they were pushing to get everything set up. So I spoke for you and said you would do it."

"OK, Billy," I said. "Fine. I'll do it. How much did you ask for?"

"I asked for $10,000. Just off the top of my head. Is that OK?"

"Just to come on stage and sing a couple of lines? Of course, that's great." Billy didn't know it, but I'd never been paid that much for a jingle before. That fee didn't include the residual checks that could last at least a couple of years.

"Thanks for understanding, Ullanda. In comparing what they pay Ray Charles, with what they're going to give you," he said, "I was afraid you'd say no."

"No problem," I said, trying to hide my excitement over the financial arrangements. "I'd love to do it."

So a few days later, the Coke people flew me to Atlanta. We moved through rehearsals without any problems and when we got to the actual live performances, everything went smoothly. Most important, the bottlers were pleased and excited over the entire production. A few weeks later, Billy phoned again. "Ullanda, Coke is setting up another extravaganza. Everything went so well in Atlanta, they want to do it again—in New York—at Radio City Music Hall. Ray Charles will be back. They'll use the Rockettes and jingle singers. And you know what? All of them—every one of the top Coke execs—wants *you* to do this spot again. I know you're busy, but please, please, can you do this? Please say you will"

"I'd be happy to do it." I had learned to sound professional, but inside I could hardly contain the pure joy from being asked by Coke to perform again.

Coca Cola threw a huge party after the New York extravaganza. While chatting there with Billy, I told him, "This is what makes life worth living. This is the most exciting time of my life, and I love every minute of it."

I believed those words.

Or more accurately, I needed to believe my words. I was going through another period of examining my life, and doubts had begun to creep in again.

• • •

During the early 1980s, when my career was still rising, I had met some people I thought were the most fascinating in the world. For example, a fur designer in New York asked his best customers to show his products, and since I'd bought a number of his furs, he invited me to model some of his after-five wear. Most of those who agreed to model were important in the industry. It especially impressed me that the furrier was Caucasian, and the show included a variety of racial types as models.

At rehearsal, I met Mae Pang, and we struck up an instant friendship. Mae is Asian, about five feet, five with beautiful black hair down to her waist. Friendliness and sweetness poured out from her. As we talked, she mentioned that she was in the music business, but didn't say much about herself.

At the same fashion show, I met Attallah Shabazz. Just as with Mae, it was one of those moments of instant friendship. Within minutes Attallah and I were chatting as if we had known each other for years. We're both Black and were both born in October. No matter what subject came up, we seemed to feel the same way. Attallah was tall, thin, and beautiful, with finely etched features and a light complexion. Her green eyes and blondish-brown hair made her stand out. Talking to her for the first time, I could tell she was knowledgeable and well-educated. But more than that, I liked her sweetness and vibrancy.

Mae, Attallah, and I had a wonderful time getting to know one another and simply enjoying each other's company. Before the show was over, the three of us exchanged phone numbers and in the months that followed, Mae, Attallah, and I became close friends

Only later did I find out the background of these two new friends. Mae had been John Lennon's "girlfriend" after he and his wife, Yoko Ono, separated. As strange as it seems to Westerners, instead of letting John go out with just any woman, Yoko chose Mae for him to live with during their separation.

When we met, Mae had published a book about her relationship with John Lennon. She was trying to promote it, but Yoko brought a lot of pressure on the media to discredit the book. She charged that Mae was one of those groupie types who followed celebrities around and that she hadn't been important in Lennon's life. "Now I think she used me, both of them," Mae confided to me. "Since she no longer needed me, she cast me out of John's life." The adverse publicity hurt Mae, because she had really cared about John Lennon and she liked Yoko too.

Mae needed a friend, somebody to talk to, and I tried to be that friend. The more she told me, the worse I felt she had been treated, and I felt her pain with her.

As the three of us got closer, we spent a lot of time together. They came to visit me, although I never was invited to Attallah's home.

I didn't know anything about Attallah when we met and though we grew close, I still didn't learn much about her for she was an extremely private person. Though well-educated, she never tried to impress me with her background. "You know," I finally said, "I still don't know much about you. What work do you do? I don't even know where you live."

"I live in Harlem," she said. "And I produce plays. I write a little, too."

"You write your own plays?"

She nodded. "I'm involved in a company that does plays about leaders in the civil rights movement."

"Really? How did you get involved in that?"

"Through my father. He's dead now, but he used to be very much into politics and civil rights."

"Really? Did I ever hear of him? Who was your father?"

"Malcolm X."

I could hardly believe what she was telling me. I stared at her, and then I realized how much she resembled the pictures I'd seen of her father.

"I know you didn't become my friend because you knew I'm the daughter of a famous man," she told me. "It is so refreshing to have a friend who likes me just for being myself."

Then she opened up, and I learned quite a lot about her.

If anything, once I knew the background of these two women,

we became closer. Mae and Attallah needed friends who accepted them as themselves. Even if they didn't want to hear it, I felt honored to be their friend and told them. I wanted to be there when they needed to talk or just to relax.

"I can be myself around you," Attallah once said, and I felt it was the best compliment she could give me.

The three of us often went shopping together and did a lot of fun things with each other. Our relationship was warm and we could laugh and joke at things around us, and most times even act a little crazy. *

• • •

As for my personal life, I was involved with the man I wanted to marry. Some days—when I thought about it—I wondered when he would marry me. He kept putting off setting a date, saying, "Just give me time. I'm not ready for marriage." I was patient because I cared for him. He was faithful to me and didn't run around with other women. But I wanted a marriage and a home.

That was the one troublesome part of my life. My career, however, continued to spiral upward.

Then in 1983, I lost my grandfather, Alexander Jones.

My granddad had provided the strong link to my childhood, and he was the person who had taught me the most about God. He was the founder and pastor of Jones Temple in Detroit.

In the fall of 1980 came the first terrible news—Grandfather Jones had bone cancer. Surgeons amputated his right foot but it wasn't enough, for the disease had already spread. Later they took off most of his leg. In spite of his constant pain, Granddad remained thankful to be alive, and I don't think he ever complained.

It became increasingly difficult for him to stand up to preach and many times he would sit down as soon as he finished speaking. The last time I saw him, when I visited Detroit in early 1982, he had stopped driving his car. He had to hire a man to

---

* Attallah now lives in California, and we stay in touch. Mae is married, has a family, and devotes much of her time to being a homemaker. She and I are still friends.

drive him to church because he was so weak. In his tired-but-loving voice, he reminded me "Ullanda, don't ever forget that God loves you."

"Yes, Granddad, I hear you." That was the one thing I didn't want him to talk about. I hadn't been to church in nearly 14 years. The less I heard about God the easier it was not to think about church, God, and my early upbringing.

Then came the call from Aunt Helen. "He passed away during the night," she said.

Though the news hit me hard, I felt a strong sense of relief. *No more suffering*, I thought. *His pain is finally over*. Part of my relief may have come from guilt. I hadn't been to see him for at least a year. So I went on with my life but I couldn't get over my own sense of loss. Although I'd long ago thrown off any pretext of being a Christian, I felt that his death took something special out of my life. Granddad had been the pillar of the family, the one who had held the family together.

My grandfather's death ended a significant part of my life. All of us wore white to the funeral as a way to celebrate his victorious life. His death was a terrible loss.

But I didn't think too much about his death or his lingering influence in my life.

That would come later.

Chapter 2

Granddad's death pushed my thoughts backward to my childhood. Sitting through his funeral and standing beside his grave, I squeezed my eyes shut against the memories. I wished I could erase a number of them from my life, but they were part of me.

Our next-door neighbor is one of my few early-childhood memories. Both our mama and daddy were gone a lot, especially at night, leaving us children at home by ourselves. There were five of us—my two older sisters and my two baby brothers. The Caucasian woman next door treated us kindly. She had no family and seemed to enjoy our company—for a while. When we were hungry, we'd go over there and she would feed us. I can remember several times, late at night—perhaps 10:00—and Mom still hadn't come home. Scared of the dark, we'd race to our neighbor's house and pound on her front door.

Looking back, I realize we must have been a burden on her, but she didn't complain. She took us in and made us feel welcome. Once after feeding us, she said, "You children have to talk to your parents and make sure they are taking care of you. This is not right."

"Yes, ma'am," Sonja, my older sister, said. We decided not to go back for a while.

But our folks still didn't come home nights, and we stayed by ourselves most of the time. Probably not more than a couple of weeks passed before we started going to our neighbor's house again.

I think I was the one who said to the others, "You know if

she thought we were different children, we wouldn't have any problem. We'd go over there and she would give us what we asked for."

We talked about this for a while, then one of us said, "Well, why don't we try to look White like her? Then she wouldn't know who we were."

The next thing I knew we had gotten into Mom's bath powder. We patted it all over our faces and hands.

"Got to fix our hair too," said Verbena.

"Then she really won't know who we are," I said. Once we agreed that we all looked White, we went over and knocked on her door. "Why, look at you children." She started to laugh. "Who are you?"

"We just wanted to know if you had any food you would give some poor White orphan children," I said.

"We're awful hungry," Verbena said, "and we have walked a long way."

"Come in, come in," she said. She brought us inside and fed us. Then she went into the other room. We didn't know she was calling the juvenile authorities, but we could hear her voice. "I have three children who live next door, and their parents are never home. Can you come and get them? I'm sure their parents will pick them up tomorrow, but this has been going on for months, and I'm concerned that their parents are never home to look after them."

A short time later, two people came to the house and said, "We'd like you to come with us." They weren't mean looking, and we knew we had to go, even though we didn't understand exactly what was happening.

We must have been a sight, with our dark faces covered with white powder. We all piled into the back of one car and they took us to the juvenile detention center.

Once there, somebody took each of us into a small room and cleaned us up, washing off all the powder and making sure we were clean and presentable. They gave us cotton gowns to put on and said, "You'll sleep here tonight."

"But we want to go home," I insisted.

"You'll have to stay here tonight," the woman said. "You can go home tomorrow."

They led us into a room filled with bunk beds. I don't re-member if there were other children there or not. I know we all cried a lot. I was worried that Mother would come home and not find any of us and be worried.

I could just barely see out the window, but I sat on the bed and stared through the glass, unable to see anything but dark-ness. *What is going to happen to us?* I kept wondering. Were they going to take us away from our parents? Send us away to some terrible place?

By then we had become thoroughly confused, and we thought that since our parents hadn't come yet, they'd left us for-ever. Verbena started to cry and then I cried. Soon all of us were crying. We'd fall asleep, then wake up a short time later and start crying again. Morning finally came. We were sent to a room to be vaccinated, but before we got to the head of the line, a woman came to get us. "Your mother and father have come," she said. "And she's very upset that you're here."

When we heard that, we grabbed each other and began to cry again.

"I'm sorry, so sorry, so sorry," Mother kept saying. "I didn't know she would send you to the juvenile home." But she also re-minded us, "You know you weren't supposed to bother that nice lady any more."

They took us home, and we felt ashamed for having embar-rassed them. At the time it didn't occur to us that they had ne-glected or failed us.

* * *

My mother, Sally Jones McCullough, and my dad separated when I was 6 years old. I loved my dad and I missed him after he moved out. He kept in contact with us, but it wasn't the same as having him in the house with us. Although I was too young to un-derstand the problems between them, I have the impression that they had been unhappy for a long, long time before they separated.

I remember Mother as unhappy and lonely, then my father started drinking. Later Mother began to drink too. Occasionally they still attended Grandfather Jones's church. Before I was born, my father, Clyde McCullough, played the organ, and my mother played the piano. Both sang in the choir. By the time we children came along, however, they'd slowly drifted away from church activities.

Their separation meant that my mother had to go to work. Unfortunately, she had no particular skills, so had a difficult time getting work. Finally she found a job as a clerk in a boutique. My father worked as a librarian at the main public library in Detroit.

Shortly after they separated and Mom started working, my aunt, Helen Jones, became one of the most important people of my life. Aunt Helen was 18 years old and still lived with my grandparents.

"I'd like to take care of Ullanda," Aunt Helen said, taking my hand. "She can live with me, and she'll be there any time you want her."

Mother agreed. I'm not sure why, but I've always assumed that Sonja and Verbena were old enough to take care of themselves, and my two brothers were so young they needed constant care. Aunt Helen lived in the home of strict Pentecostal parents, and she wasn't particularly outgoing. I'm sure she enjoyed having me with her.

Helen thought of herself as the "black duckling" of the family. This may be difficult for those outside the Black culture to understand, but she felt sad because she was the darkest of the children. She got teased about it regularly. In the Black community, color of skin is a big issue. This goes back to the days of slavery. The light-colored slaves were brought into the house to work, and the darker ones went into the fields. This color distinction reflected the fact that the light-toned slaves had been born to slave women by their White owners. Even today some people think that the lighter their skin, the better they are.

Consequently, because the other 11 Jones children were fairer, Aunt Helen felt she was looked down on, and thus she felt inferior. At that time she had but little self-assurance and felt concerned over her brown complexion. She is about five foot, five, quite thin, with attractive, Indian-like features and a reddish brown skin tone. She was very giving—that's how I saw her then and still think of her today. "I like to make you happy," she said to me once.

When I was 6, I went to live with Aunt Helen and my grandparents, staying with them until I was 9. By then, my mother was divorced and a short time later, William Walker, who became our stepfather, moved in.

I liked William. He was a hard-working man. He held down two jobs, and he provided for us as if we were his own children. We kids decided that any man who would take on a family of five children and a woman who had very little, must be really wonderful. And he was good to us, although he wasn't around much because of his work. At the same time, my father still paid child support and whatever extra my mom needed, he gladly gave if he could. Although they were divorced, I don't think my dad ever stopped loving my mother.

Maybe that troublesome childhood explains why I enjoyed the three years I lived with them. Grandfather's house was a beautiful, large, brick house on a corner lot. It had four levels—a basement, main level, upstairs, and the attic that they had converted into an apartment. We had a beautiful yard with a huge pine tree out front. My grandmother loved landscaping and flowers, so she had flowers everywhere. I thought that being at Grandfather's house was almost as good as being in heaven.

Helen made my clothes for school. They were pretty and well-made, but they did cause problems. She liked plaids and pleated skirts—nice-looking, conservative-style clothes. Some of my classmates made fun of me because they thought I was trying to dress up and look better than they did.

I went to school in a tough Black neighborhood, about a mile from Aunt Helen's. It was in a different, lower-economic neighborhood and in my "fancy" clothes, I didn't fit in.

I finally said, "Aunt Helen, I don't like being dressed this way and wearing my hair all fixed up. The kids make fun of me."

"That's OK. Don't worry about them. You just look nice for yourself. You go on and dress the way you are."

I didn't stop there, of course. Sometimes I'd cry or plead with her, but it didn't do any good. I recall wanting a pair of pointed-toed boots like the other kids wore. When I coaxed my father into buying me a pair, Aunt Helen made him take them back.

Tears. Pleas. No matter what I said, it didn't make any differ-ence. Aunt Helen replaced them with penny loafers. Naturally, I hated them. I cried, pointed out how awful they looked, insisted they didn't fit right, and howled that everyone would laugh at me.

"Ullanda, you're still just a child, and you don't know what you're doing," she said. "You'll have to trust me and let me rear you in the way that will be best for you."

Now I realize what she was trying to teach me. If she had put it into words, she would have said, "Ullanda, in order to make it in this life you have to take the necessary steps. You have to dress a certain way, you have to look a certain way, you have to be educated." She dressed me for the neighborhood I lived in and not for where I went to school. She also reminded me that my grandfather was the pastor, and everyone looked up to him. "You have to dress in a way that brings glory to God."

Deep within, even then, I felt alone and different. And sad.

Many years would pass before I found healing for those feel-ings. After I'd grown and moved to New York, I was so thankful that Aunt Helen had taught me style and how to get good value from the clothes I wore. She also helped me learn to stand up for myself when others were against me.

She taught me a lot!

Chapter 3

. . . .

*U*llanda," Aunt Helen said matter-of-factly, "you have to go back home and live with your parents."

"But why, Aunt Helen? I like it here. Have I been bad?"

"No, you have been a good little girl." Her voice was sad, and I knew something was wrong. "You need to be back with your family."

I was 9 years old, and although I didn't know everything, I knew about babies. Aunt Helen was not married and she was pregnant. She didn't have to tell me for I overheard her and my grandparents discussing it.

Her parents loved her and would never have sent her away, but she had hurt and disappointed them. Now they decided I needed to go home so Helen could take care of her own child.

But I could think only that I was going back to the small house she'd taken me out of. I was also naive enough that I didn't understand how she could be pregnant and not married. It was a terrible blow to me. I felt rejected and I couldn't hold back the tears. But I knew my broken heart wouldn't change anything. Even my mother agreed that the best thing for me to do was to come home. "You see, Ullanda," Mom said, "Aunt Helen will soon have her own child to take care of." So Aunt Helen packed up my things and took me back to my mother.

Although I loved being at the Jones's house, I was always thrilled to see my family. When I returned, they treated me the same as before, so there wasn't much of an adjustment. But their lifestyle was radically different. While living with Aunt Helen, we went to church several times a week. By contrast, my family merely went now and then.

In my grandparents' home, we had a strict family structure. We ate meals together and always at a certain time. Everything was done in an orderly way and everybody cooperated nicely. Looking back, I would say that we bonded at my grandfather's house and were a true family—exactly what I didn't have in my own home.

Unstructured and fragmented was the way our home operated. We didn't see a lot of William during the week because he worked so many hours. Mother worked all day. Many times she came home exhausted from being on her feet all day. Or she wouldn't even come home until late at night. Sonja had already learned to do most of the cooking, and Verbena was learning as well. I took on chores that I hadn't had to do at my grandparent's.

After I moved back, my mother insisted that we three girls, at least, attend church, although that's about the time she stopped going. She would say, "I want to spend time with William." Because of his long work hours, Sunday morning was one of the few times they were able to be together. I think also that Mom was quite dependent on William and needed more from him than he was able to give.

It didn't do any good to go to Dad. He had moved in with his mother. Sometimes he picked us up and took us to events such as the Ice Capades, the zoo, or exhibition games by the Globe Trotters. Then his mother died from cancer. I don't know if it was the loss of his family and then the death of his mother, but what ever happened, he began to drink heavily, which made him inaccessible to us. About then, or perhaps a little later, Mom started to drink, too, although William never did. He just wasn't around enough to have much influence on us.

"I'm just so unhappy," Mom said once when I asked her why she was drinking. "William isn't here, and I never get to see him, and I'm lonely all the time."

"I'm here, Mom," I said.

"I know," she said and patted my cheek. "But it's not the same thing. I need William around me, but he's always working,

working, working."

William worked hard and wanted to make sure he provided for whatever we needed. She complained about his being gone, and yet he took care of us.

Then Mom changed jobs and began to work as a bartender. I think that being in that environment encouraged her to drink. None of us was happy about her new job, and everything seemed to be getting worse. It has been many years and my memory may not be totally accurate, but I know our house wasn't a happy place to grow up.

Particularly I remember that most week nights during the week, not only were both of them gone, but often we had no food in the house. Caught up in her own personal misery, I don't think Mom realized how difficult she made life for us. Fortunately, we could go to a small grocery store near our house. I don't remember the owners name, but he was very kind to us. He knew our grandfather well, and may even have been a member of his church.

"Just take what you need," he would say. "Don't worry about paying. I'll get the money." He would write down our purchases and give us all the credit we needed. Later my mother or Dad went to the store and paid. I don't think it bothered Mom that we had to go over there so often.

The situation got worse. Soon we made daily trips to the grocery store. We seldom saw Mom. She came home to sleep and bathe, and then went back out again.

Despite all the problems I faced after going back home, one good thing came out of it. I started singing. I had done a few solos in grandfather's church, but I didn't think of that as real singing. Since my uncles and aunts attended and all were musical, I had no sense of doing anything unusual.

It started when I got to be friends with Doris Jackson. She and her family went to my grandfather's church. One day Doris and I tried to sing together, and we harmonized quite well. Then Phyllis Metcalf, who lived down the street, joined us, and we formed a trio.

We sounded good together, at least I thought so. Harmonizing with Doris and Phyllis provided an escape from my loneliness and sadness. When we practiced together, I could forget about Mom's drinking and the arguments between her and William. I could forget that we didn't have parents at home to take care of us.

Singing also carried over into school, for Doris, Phyllis, and I were in the same class. Occasionally, when we finished our lessons early, our teacher asked us to sing. The other kids really applauded us. I loved feeling I had done something well and I liked being noticed and appreciated for our singing. Since everyone enjoyed it, we thought we must be pretty good. We practiced together a lot and sang for any kind of event that we were asked to.

One day in music class, our teacher, Mrs. Helen Woods, was teaching us tunes from *The Sound of Music*. The rest of the class was having trouble with the parts but, without even realizing it, I was on key and singing well. Finally, the teacher raised her hand and told everyone to stop singing. Then she called me to the front of the room. She had me sing the notes for the first two lines until the other students could hear what it should sound like. Then she told me to sing the entire piece. "I want the rest of you to listen to her," she told the class. "Blend your voices with hers. Stay right with her."

She asked me to stay after class that day. My heart pounded with apprehension, but I stayed. To my surprise, she told me that I had a beautiful singing voice and the potential to do something important with it. She wanted to give me private voice lessons.

Two mornings a week I sang for 20 to 25 minutes with her. She taught me to do solo work, but that confused me. I didn't know I could sing solo parts and wasn't interested in learning how because I loved to harmonize. I did what she asked. However, I didn't have much interest in the sessions.

She wanted me to learn to sing classical music, but the influence of pop music was too strong. Actually, she did something quite helpful to me that would aid in my career. She started teaching me how to read music and to sight sing—to sing just from looking at the printed notes.

Mrs. Woods was very much into opera and kept pushing me to do that kind of singing. Even though I wasn't interested, I couldn't say that to a teacher. We had been brought up to respect authority. But I couldn't hide the expression on my face from her, and I'm sure she knew how I really felt.

"You can learn," she insisted. "You have the capability. Just try, please. I see something in you that is pure talent. You have to pursue this, to give yourself a chance."

She was a strict disciplinarian, too, and wouldn't allow me to cheat and give less than my best. A few times I tried to depend on my ear instead of reading the notes, but she was too clever for me. "Read, Ullanda. *Read the notes.*"

"Yes, ma'am," I would answer, wishing I didn't have to be with her.

"You have to do this, Ullanda, for yourself and because of the gift you have."

After a few weeks of working with me, Mrs. Woods came bursting into the classroom where I was waiting for her. "Ullanda, I have special, wonderful news for you." She said that a friend of hers—a famous opera singer from Europe—was coming to Detroit. He had agreed to listen to me sing. "He can do wonderful things for you if he thinks you have the talent," she told me.

I tried to be enthusiastic for her sake, but I really didn't care. When he came, she had him sing for the whole school in the auditorium. After the concert, he was going to listen to me. I remember he was Black, a very large, tall man with a powerful voice. Even I recognized how talented he was.

I was sure I couldn't sing a note.

"Relax," he said in his deep bass voice. He smiled. "You don't have anything to worry about."

When I finished singing he turned to Mrs. Woods and started to talk to her as if I weren't in the room. "Yes, she is talented," he said. "I would be interested in teaching her, but I'll really have to work on her vibrato. She does have a problem with vibrato."

I had no idea what he meant so he explained further, talking about the number of sound waves in my vibrato. I still didn't understand what he was saying.

"Oh, that will be no problem," Mrs. Woods said, as her face filled with joy. "I want you to teach her."

A few minutes later it was settled that I would take lessons.

When I told my family that a famous opera singer had agreed to give me lessons, Grandmother McCullough said she would pay for them. She insisted that Sonja have the benefit of the lessons as well. We went to his studio in his house for three months. He worked with me on my sight-singing skills. He concentrated first on teaching me how to read music, and then how to sing the scale properly—all the basics that good voice teachers go through. Because I had been depending on my ear all along, the discipline he demanded was hard.

"It's just too much work," I would say to Sonja. She felt the same way. Of course I needed everything he taught. I just wasn't smart enough to realize it.

I did what he told me, and he must have improved my vibrato. But I had no idea how much benefit I was getting from him. If only I had had enough sense to grasp what an invaluable opportunity he was offering me. But it was too late for him to have a lasting effect. By then my eyes had a different vision. I was going to become a Motown singer. Motown, founded in Detroit, was *the* pop record label. For me, there just wasn't anything else.

In the years ahead, I had to learn my lesson the hard way.

After three months, the singer went back to Germany to tour with a new opera production and my lessons stopped. I rejoined my two girlfriends, and soon we were back into pop singing.

Then came an exciting time in my life. I knew my big chance had arrived. I was going to get the opportunity to audition for Motown records.

Chapter 4

• • • • • • • • • • • • • • • • • • • •

e can do it," Sonja said. "Just sign up. That's all we have to do, and they'll listen to us. Once they hear us, we're in."

She had to convince me. I'd heard the same radio ads about the talent search and people thought I was good, but I knew my weaknesses. At 13, I didn't feel I was good enough to sing in front of a live audience. But Mrs. Woods, and then the opera singer, had been giving me those voice lessons. "All right," I said, as a wave of excitement began to stir in me. "I'll do it." I was ambitious, and I just knew this was the break I needed.

Shortly after the opera teacher moved back to Europe, Sonja, Verbena, and I formed a sister group and sang most of the Motown hits. We wanted to be like the Motown recording artists—the Marvelettes, Mandelas, Temptations, Marvin Gaye, and Tammy Turrel all combined, but most of all, the Supremes. They were the hottest female trio in the music field, singing middle-of-the-road pop music. Best of all, they sang on the Motown label and recorded in Detroit.

In those days, Motown sponsored an annual talent contest that got enormous publicity through the media and anyone could sign up. Sonja had already decided that she and I would be part of the new talent that the contest would discover. At that time I was dancing on a weekly TV program called *Swinging Time*, a program much like American Bandstand, a favorite among the kids I knew. They filmed it over in Ontario, Canada, which was only five minutes from downtown Detroit by going through the tunnel. On the program we danced to canned music.

I became a regular because a friend named John Collins wrote in and got tickets to attend and try out, and invited me to go with him. Once they saw that we could really dance, they asked us to be regulars on the show. We never got any money for it but they paid our travel expenses. It was fun dancing with a lot of others to the Motown hits.

But singing was different from dancing and I always felt a little self-conscious before an audience. And even though I wanted to perform, I was scared of people staring at me. However, since Sonja had decided we were going to compete in the Motown contest, I agreed to be part of it.

Not that I noticed at the time, but our interest in Motown music took so much time that it slowly pulled me away from gospel music and the church. My sisters had long been skipping church, and now I didn't go often either. And now I had myself convinced that I was going to get my big chance. Verbena didn't sing as well as Sonja and I did—and she knew her limitations—so we decided to go as soloists.

We mailed in our application cards and waited.

When we got word of a time and date to audition, we just knew we were on the brink of success. The news reported that about 500 people had signed up but that didn't discourage us.

"We're going to audition for Motown!" We told our friends. "Isn't this great?"

We had about a month to get ready, and the closer it got to the time, the more enthusiastic we became. Our family was excited too. My mother had often pushed me to sing for people, but this audition was different. This was a *real* talent show.

"You are going to win," Mom said. "Oh, both of you can do it. You can. I know you can."

At the Fox Theater, they told us they auditioned female singers by age groups which put Sonja and me in different categories. Both Sonja and I were sent to a room labeled "Female Solo." We sat on long rows of chairs with other young women and waited.

I looked around while listening to instructions given by the man in charge. The other dozen or so teenagers looked so self-assured and mature. What little confidence I had before I went in, left me.

One by one a girl was called to perform. I soon realized that they were doing more than listening to voices. They tried to confuse the singers to see how they'd perform under pressure. Several of the girls burst into tears and ran from the room.

I knew I wouldn't give in to tears, but I was scared. "I'll never get through this," I whispered to Sonja.

"Yes, you will. You'll be fine." She lowered her voice even more and laid on the big-sister advice. "Whatever you do, don't stop singing until they tell you to stop. You know the song. Don't let the other music confuse you. You can do it."

The longer I waited, the more nervous I became. Finally I heard, "Ullanda McCullough!" My nerves were shot and I shrieked, "Here!"

Sonja whispered, "It's OK, baby, it's OK. You can do it. Don't worry."

But I was nervous and I suppose it showed.

I sang exactly seven words.

"Thank you. That's enough," the man said. "Thank you for coming."

That was it. That was my audition. My big chance. Seven words and I was finished. Years later when I could laugh about it, I told friends, that was the end of my Motown career as a soloist.

A few days later, Sonja who had done very well, got called back for the next round of auditions. She was, quite naturally, even more excited. "I'm in, I'm in," she kept saying. "Just think I could stand up there and sing on the same stage as Stevie Wonder."

She really believed it.

So did I. So did the rest of the family.

But it didn't happen. After her second audition, she never heard from them again. So that was the end of Sonja's career with Motown.

Ironically, I did appear on the final program—but not as a singer. The Motown people asked the producers of *Swinging Time* to choose three of their best couples to dance on stage for the grand opening of the program. John Collins and I were one of the couples chosen. I had a wonderful time. I'd been dancing on

Swinging Time for three or four months, so this was no big deal.

After the show, we had the opportunity to meet the professional entertainers. I wanted to meet Stevie Wonder, but I couldn't build up the courage to go up to him and introduce myself.*

I was 13 years old, and I thought my singing career was over.

Soon Motown memories were left behind. The three of us continued to sing together but we didn't much think about a career in music. We just enjoyed singing. Still young, school took up a lot of my time, and I loved math, drama, and sports. But singing was really what I wanted to do most.

• • •

Easter was the one time that we all went to church, even Mother. Huge hats with large flowers were much in style then and Mother, a beautiful woman anyway, looked outstanding. People simply turned and stared in admiration when she walked into a room. Easter, 1967, is the one I remember most—for it led to one of the saddest times in my teenaged years. We all wore new clothes and were proud of the way we looked.

But that Easter Sunday Sonja met a young man named William and she fell head-over-heels in love. "He is so cute," she must have told us 10 times a day. He made it obvious that he liked her too. Sonja thought that William was the greatest, smartest, and best looking guy she'd ever seen. Because he was active in church and Sonja wanted to be near him, she started going to church all the time too.

Then Sonja began to change, and I didn't like it. Until then, music had been everything to her but it became obvious that she was losing interest. "I don't want to sing today," she said a little too often.

"Oh, come on," I begged. "We can cut it short if you like."

"Not this time," she'd say. The next thing I knew, I'd hear her on the telephone having a lengthy conversation with William.

Frankly, I didn't understand her attraction to him. Not that

---

*Later, when I was established in the jingle business, my dream did come true—I met Stevie Wonder.

he wasn't a nice person, but she could have had just about any boy her age. Sonja had been extremely popular in school. Among other things—and this was a predominately Polish school—the girls chose her as head cheerleader. Everybody loved her. Sonja had been my idol, and I wanted to be just like her. Pretty and popular, all kinds of boys wanted to date her. I even coveted her beautiful voice. But suddenly my wonderful, older sister had changed.

I could put up with her not wanting to practice as much as we did. But things grew more serious. Before long she didn't seem to want to do anything in her free time except to be with William. Naturally, Verbena and I became concerned and took our hurt out on William, blaming him for taking our sister away from us.

William was handsome, no question about that. Tall and clean cut, he was the type we called conservative. By that we meant that he never got into the "hip" way of dressing or showed any interest in Motown music. He didn't have his hair slicked down or wear the popular pointed-toe shoes. He worked with his father in some kind of machine shop and had lost one arm. At our young, insensitive age, we'd say, "Sonja, when you can have any guy around, why do you settle for William?"

"Because he's the best of them all," she'd say in a dreamy voice.

I think I would have liked William if I hadn't hated him for taking Sonja away from our world of fun. Back then, I couldn't understand my sister at all. Verbena, our friends, and I were busy playing cool and hip, and she was turning away from everything we thought was important. She started to dress more conservatively and showed less and less interest in Motown music. Something was wrong with her, and I told her so.

"I'm fine," she told me with a cheerful smile. "I like what's happening in my life. I've never been this happy before."

"Happy?" I shrieked. "I think you're out of your mind. But it's your mind you lost and not mine."

"One day you'll understand," she said. I didn't like to hear that either. Now and then we'd talked about keeping our sister act and going professional. It hurt to have Sonja pull away from us, but she'd had an experience that changed her life. She didn't say anything, but we knew something was going on. Finally she announced, "I don't want to sing any more."

"Not sing any more?" I screamed. "Are you crazy?"

"You can't drop out like that," Verbena flatly told her.

"I'm sorry, but I'm not going to sing with you again."

I felt crushed. "How can you do this to us? How can you just walk out on us now?" I knew I was yelling, but if I hadn't yelled, I would have started to cry. Sonja was ruining my life by backing away from music. The Sonja I knew and loved had left me and another person had taken her place.

It would be years before I finally understood why she made that decision.

Chapter 5

· ·

We didn't let Sonja go without a fight, but Sonja stayed calm. "I know you don't like hearing this," Sonja told me, "and I'm sorry. I know how much singing means to you, but I can't do it any more."

"But why?" I kept demanding, the sadness and disappointment rising in my voice. "There's nothing wrong with the songs we sing or the way we dance!"

"You've been doing it for years yourself, girl," Verbena said.

"Well, I can't sing with you the way we used to. My life is different now, that's why."

"Why?" I yelled. "Why are you deserting us like this?"

"Because I've turned to Jesus Christ. I've been born again. I don't *want* those things any longer. Now I want to serve God." It seemed as if we argued and yelled at each other for at least an hour. I kept saying, "How could you do this to us? We're your sisters." It didn't occur to me to try to see things from her perspective. Sonja had ruined my dreams of becoming a famous singer and part of a sister act. To make it worse, Sonja was the best dancer and singer of us three. She picked up the routines faster than we did and showed us how to do the steps. She had the best ear and caught the slightest mistake in harmonizing.

It must have been hard on her, too. "I'm sorry," Sonja told us, trying to end the argument, "but that's how I feel. I'm a Christian now." Her voice was quiet and calm. "My values are different."

"When did you get so holy and perfect?" yelled Verbena.

"Say what you want, but I refuse to sing that kind of music."

She stood her ground and never again have I heard her sing "that kind of music."

I couldn't understand—*I didn't want to understand.*

"I've got real music in my soul now," Sonja said. "And it's the good kind."

Verbena and I decided that William was the one who had made her change. So we tried everything we could think of to break them up. "I want to tell you something else about your precious William," I remember Verbena said once, and she concocted some story that made him look bad.

But no matter what we said or did, Sonja wouldn't budge in her loyalty and commitment to him. Sonja had made up her mind. She had started down the straight and narrow road, and she refused to turn around.*

Once Sonja quit, it was over. Verbena and I stopped trying to sing like the Supremes.

• • •

We lived in the section of Detroit called Hamtramck until I finished junior high. Then we moved into a simple home in Coney Gardens, an upper-middle-class neighborhood. The front of the building was a drugstore, and we rented the living quarters behind. It had a huge back yard and a great view—it was almost as nice as Granddad's house.

I especially liked my new school, Pershing High. At that time, the school was 60 percent Black and the rest Caucasian, and I don't recall any racial incidents. All of us McCulloughs made a lot of friends at school. Later Mom bought a nice brick home in the same area.

I joined the chorus at Pershing High. My teacher was Robert Harris. I liked him a lot even though he was very much into opera and other types of high brow music. He was Black and well-educated. I didn't know that highly educated Black men were interested in those kind of things.

I took a class in Black history so I could understand more

_____

* Sonja married William. Today he's a minister in the Church of God of Christ.

about my heritage. After learning the many wonderful accomplishments of my race, I felt good about being Black. I've since learned that a Caucasian slave owner on my father's side is part of our family tree. The family tells me that my paternal grandfather looked like a an Irishman, and my grandmother had Cherokee blood. This mixed heritage has helped me see why my father used to teach us to love everyone no matter what their color or background.

A few weeks into my first year of high school, Mr. Harris told me that I had real possibilities for a musical career, and urged me to think seriously about my singing. What I most appreciated about him was that he tried to work with most of us individually. I'll never forget one thing he told me. "I think you have a gift to sing," he said.

My mother had always told me that.

"Wow, really? You really mean that?"

"Absolutely."

Can this really be true? I wondered. Mrs. Woods and the opera singer had believed it and Mom was convinced I could sing. Mr. Harris offered me almost every female solo part that came up, but each time I held back. I explained to him that I didn't much like doing solos, but preferred to harmonize.

"You can do that too," he assured me, "but you have a gift, and I want to help you use it. I'll give you private lessons."

I'll never forget him for encouraging me in that way, but back then I wasn't interested. I did let him give me voice lessons a few times but my heart wasn't in it and he realized that.

But he didn't give up. At least once a week, he would find some way to encourage me. "Ullanda, whatever happens, don't give up. Use your talent."

● ● ●

That fall I joined drama class at school. At the end of the year, the teacher gave me an award for being the best all-around musician, singer, or soloist for the drama class. I began to think, *Wow, I've been given this award because they think I did the best job. Maybe I do have some talent after all.*

I was finally learning to believe in myself.

Both my mother and father tried to help me accept myself and my talent. Despite their personal problems, both were enthusiastic about anything we children did. At first Mom had pushed Sonja just as much as she did me. But once Sonja became a Christian and flatly refused to do any more singing, Mom left her alone. Another part of Mom, I think, was thrilled at Sonja's change of direction, but she never said a lot about it.

Mom didn't say much about my having a career in music, but I think she saw music as my way out of Detroit. Maybe it was also her way of living her own unfulfilled dreams through me. Whatever her motives, she pushed me into every opportunity to sing—in my classroom, in the neighborhood, or wherever a door opened.

When we were younger, I still remember the times she invited neighbors over so I could entertain them. Once they were seated, Mom would say, "OK, Bunny.* Sing for them. Show them how pretty you can sing."

I didn't have enough confidence for that, however, and I'd tell her, "I don't want to sing alone in front of these people. I like to sing in groups. I don't like singing solo." I liked to sing with others because I loved harmonizing. The beauty of harmonized music sounded prettier to me than my voice by itself. Also, I didn't like the feeling of people watching me, and when I was with a group I didn't feel eyes focused on just me.

Yet I couldn't get away from Mom's bright-eyed expectation and pride in my voice.

So I sang.

Later, when I started moving ahead in the music business, Mom loved getting dressed up and going out to see the different shows where I performed. Every chance she had, Mom would go to concerts where I sang. She was more star-struck than I ever was. And, quite naturally, I hated having a star-struck mother around.

"Mom, do you have to come with me?" I asked several times. "You know how kids are. You embarrass me. Why do you have to be here? You're a mother and not a young person."

"I like watching you, Bunny," she'd tell me. "I'm proud of you."

_____
* a childhood nickname

Even though I tried to get her to stay away, she helped me tremendously by pushing me. I probably wouldn't have done it on my own. As an adult, I can now realize she was part of the force behind my drive to succeed.

When I started my senior year in the fall of 1967, I was still dancing on *Swinging Time*. One reason the weekly show meant so much to me was because home wasn't very happy and dancing helped me forget all my concerns. By then Sonja had married William. Verbena married, had a baby, and then separated from her husband. They soon developed a pattern of breaking up and getting back together. I went to school, performed fairly often, and danced on *Swinging Time*. When *Swinging Time* went off the air I became an "ordinary" high school kid again. Only weeks later, I met a classmate named Pam Vincent. She would change the direction of my life.

Chapter 6

. . . .

Though normally a shy person, Pam Vincent walked up to me at school one day and introduced herself. "I know who you are," she said, when I told her my name. "I used to watch you on *Swinging Time*. And I think you were one of the best dancers on the program!"

From the beginning, Pam and I hit it off just great. We were both seniors—a common ground for friendship—but most of all, I liked her sincerity. And though she was sweet and caring, she had few friends. Pam didn't get involved in school activities, but stayed to herself a lot.

For me, the depth of our friendship began when Pam overheard a conversation between me and the clerk at the school office. Pam had just paid for her senior graduation pictures, and I was in line behind her. The clerk told me that unless I had the money to pay for my pictures by the end of the week, the pictures would be sent back. There was no way I could have the money by then, but I didn't want to admit that. I was turning away in despair, when Pam offered to loan me the money to pay for them. At first I refused, but she insisted that $33.75 was no big deal for her and that I could pay her back later.

I was overwhelmed to think that she cared enough to loan me the money. None of my other friends would have done that. Eventually I paid her back, and even then it was obvious it hadn't been a big thing for her. Our friendship grew even closer.

As I grew to know her better, I was puzzled by the fact that she always had money to use as she wanted or needed. "How can you afford this?" I asked the first time I saw her car, a red, two-door, year-old-model Ford. "You're only in high school. I know your parents aren't rich or anything."

She played it cool. "Oh, I have a job," she said, and wouldn't say anything more.

I had grown to love Pam, and didn't worry about the mystery of her money. And then, all of a sudden, it was solved. Pam was driving me home and the car radio played softly in the background. She reached over and turned up the volume. "That's me," she said.

"What do you mean, that's you?"

"That's me singing on the radio."

"That's not you on the radio. Give me a break." I started to laugh. "Don't you think I recognize Freda Payne singing? Come on, that's not you."

"Yes, it is Freda Payne, but I'm singing backup." She paused. "Ullanda, that's what I do. That's how I make so much money. You keep asking me what I do, well, this is what I do for a living. I sing background for different recording artists."

"Are you serious? You get paid to do that?"

"Yes, that's what I do."

"Man, that's exciting," I said. "How did you get into this? How long have you been doing it? Who are the people you sing for."

Pam laughed at my questions and told me about some of the famous singers she and two others did background for. I could hardly believe it. I kept thinking, *Wow, she has the most wonderful job in the world.* Simply happy for my friend, it never occurred to me that she might help me break into the music business myself.

So I was surprised when she asked a month before graduation if I wanted to audition for her group.

She said that she would be leaving for college in the fall and the group would need a replacement.

"Oh, Pam, you can't be serious," I exclaimed. "I mean, I never thought—Yes! Yes! I'd love it!" I could hardly believe the offer. I'd had some vague plans about going to college in California and trying to break into the business out there.

"I'll set up an audition. It's just my sister and another woman. You come over to my house, and if you have what it takes, they'll hire you."

Dozens of questions came rattling out about preparing and various things like that. I even asked what I should wear.

Pam laughed. "Don't fuss. Don't do anything to get ready. Just come and we'll find out if you can fit in or not. That's all there is to it."

"This is great, this is great," I kept saying. "What do you call yourselves?"

"We don't have a name. It's my sister, Joyce, and me and the leader, Telma. She's the one who'll make the final decision. But don't worry about it. I know you can do it."

Pam arranged for me to come to her home one day after school. She introduced me to the two women, both of whom were about five years older, very sophisticated looking, and very attractive.

The leader was Telma Hopkins. None of us had any way of knowing that she would become a big name in music by being part of Tony Orlando and Dawn. Later she found even greater fame on television through the series, *Gimme Me a Break* and *Family Matters*. But back in 1969, she was just Telma, the leader of the group that did back-up singing for Motown's sister label, Stax Records, which was run by the former Motown producer/writer team of Holland, Dozier, and Holland.

"OK, let me audition you," Telma said in business-like fashion, "and see what you can do."

I forced myself to remain calm as I waited for her to explain what part she wanted me to do. If only they'll take me, I kept thinking . . . if only I'm good enough.

She chose a popular song and asked, "Do you know this one? You sing harmony, don't you?"

"Sure," I said. When I opened my mouth, I forgot about being jittery. They started to sing, and it was fun to join in.

After we'd gone through a full stanza, Telma stopped us. "That was pretty good," she said. Behind them, Pam was smiling. "OK, Ullanda," Telma said, "this time I'm going to sing alto, you sing soprano, and Joyce is going to sing the second."

The singing sounded really good to me. Somehow I knew then that I would fit in with them. We practiced two or three more numbers before Telma said, "OK, I think that's enough."

We sat down then, and she said, "You've got a good ear, and you can pick out parts. You can sing all right," she added. She hired me on the spot.

"Pam is going away to school in September," Joyce said, "and you can fill in for her while she's away."

I understood. They were letting me know that the position was temporary. I'd sing with them only during the school year when Pam was away.

"This is great," I kept saying. It seemed as if everything was falling into place, and I already knew what I wanted to do with my life. I would have a job before I graduated.

I began regular practices with Joyce and Telma and in the fall of 1970, Pam left for college and I was part of the group. Finally my chance came to cut a record with them. We met at a studio in Detroit where they were scheduled to record back-up for a group. Telma, Joyce, and Pam had been doing a lot of the background vocals on records for former Motown groups and producers as well as for others who came to Detroit to record. At that time, Detroit was *the* recording scene.

I can never forget the first time I went with the group to record. The man who was arranging all this said to Telma, "OK, this is the song. We want you to work up the background parts. Teach it to your group. When you've got it, we'll do it." He meant that they would record it on a separate track. Eventually, they would blend all the tracks together.

My first job with Telma and Joyce was a jingle—a commercial for a company in Detroit—that would be aired on radio. They didn't do many commercials in Detroit, so when they got an opportunity, it was a big deal.

Telma was handing me a great opportunity, and I knew it. I didn't want to blow it, but I was scared. She was strict, really a perfectionist. She had a lot of drive and demanded total concentration from herself, from Joyce, and from me. It didn't matter that I was new, she expected me to perform as well as she and Joyce did.

"We aren't trying to be good," she said once. "We are going to be known as the best group of back-up singers in the business." Even then it was easy to see that she would end up at the top of her profession. She had the talent and the drive that it took to be a success.

We worked for perhaps 20 minutes on the jingle, and I thought it sounded fine. Telma had always been patient and very nice to me in our rehearsals. She only spoke up when she felt I wasn't doing quite what she wanted.

We sang the jingle through and she stopped us. "Wait, let's do that again."

Halfway through the second time, she turned and her eyes stared into mine. "We're not blending." The niceness had gone from her voice. "Someone is off pitch on those notes." She sang them to us and explained what was wrong.

The studio people were sitting on the other side of the booth and could hear us. I felt embarrassed and nervous. Even though she was nice enough not to call names, I knew it had to be me she referred to and I felt terrible. *I'll get it right this time*, I vowed to myself.

We started again.

"No! No! Let's do it one more time. Someone's still off pitch." She stopped the tape. I think I was most conscious that the people in the engineering booth were listening to every word. I felt myself drowning in shame and embarrassment. I wanted to run out of the studio, but of course I didn't.

"All right, we'll do it again," she said and glared at me before she nodded to the production people. "This time we'll do it right."

I was trying my best. At the time, I could only take this as a personal attack. I had yet to realize that when Telma Hopkins came to the recording booth, she was totally professional and all business. Many tries later we finally got through the jingle. I was afraid she would say to the control booth something such as, "We'll come back another day when we have a better singer with us." But Telma and Joyce stayed with it until both of them liked the sound.

Suddenly it was over. When we finished, Telma was her old self again. Not one word about how badly I had done. It wasn't a personality issue, but strictly professional with her. We'd finally gotten it taped, and she was satisfied. While she and Joyce were relaxing, I could only think of all the wrong things I had done.

As we walked out, Joyce and Telma were smiling and chatting. At any second I expected Telma to say, "Ullanda, you're not working out. You're too slow to learn. Your pitch is not good enough for us. You still don't know how to blend."

But she never said it. To her credit, Telma stuck with me. Maybe it was because I was Pam's best friend. Maybe she was kind at heart. Even though she never said much to encourage me, it was when she didn't tell me I was doing something wrong that I began to realize I met her exacting standards.

I remember a few of the groups we sang for—most were groups or soloists with one or two songs that hit the top-ten on the record charts. There were no top names like the Supremes.

I was always the relief singer, however, and I wouldn't let myself forget it. Whenever Pam came home, they used her in their back-up. I often had a terrible, recurring fear that they wouldn't call me back.

But, that nightmare never happened.

Chapter 7

• •

he phone rang. It was a call from the recording studio, asking to speak to Telma. At least three times I heard her use my name.

All my insecurities came boiling to the surface. Were they asking her to get rid of me? Did they have someone else they wanted to put in my place?

This was a few months after I joined the group, and just before Pam finished her first semester at college. In fact, Pam was home visiting when the call came. The group had a recording date set for the next week and, naturally, planned to use Pam.

Telma was across the room from us, and we could hear her end of the conversation. She tried not to show it but we could tell she didn't like what she was hearing. Finally Telma said, "All right. Thanks for calling." She hung up and stared at us. The look on her face made it clear that she didn't like the message she'd gotten from Stax.

"What was that all about?" Joyce asked.

"They want a different sound," Telma said.

"What kind of different sound?" Pam asked.

"A gospel sound," she said. "Somebody there likes the timbre of Ullanda's voice. It has a gospel sound to it, it seems."

"I was brought up in a gospel church," I said.

"Well, that's the sound they want. Got it from the president himself. He told me, 'Ullanda has that sound, so make sure you use her on every recording you do for us.'" Telma was obviously unhappy over the message and over being told to use me every time. Hearing her tone, I felt she resented me because of this. And even in my shock, I understood why she would resent the demand they made and resent me for being singled out.

Since they needed only three singers for the group, this pushed Pam out of any chance to record for Stax. But for any specials they booked, or whenever they got the chance to work for a different record company, they made it quite clear they would use Pam instead of me.

Of course Pam was hurt by Stax's demand. She was my best friend, and that made it a difficult place for her to be. Finally she said, "It's all right. I'm happy for Ullanda. If that's the sound they want, that's what you have to give them. Otherwise they won't keep hiring the group, right? College is keeping me busy enough anyway."

"It's so unfair of them to do it that way," Telma said. "If they wanted the gospel sound, all they had to do was tell me. We've all had gospel backgrounds, so we could give them that."

The three of them discussed the phone call for a long time as if I weren't even there. I sat nearby, happy, yet embarrassed for feeling so good and acutely sad that I was the cause of Pam being squeezed out.

After they'd talked it all out and calmed down, Telma, ever the professional, said, "OK, Stax, you said you know what you want. That's what you'll get."

When we had a chance to be alone, I told Pam, "I'm sorry this happened."

"It's not your fault," she said. And she really meant it. She hugged me. "And it's a wonderful chance for you."

That was the quality that made Pam such a special friend.

* * *

That's how I got into the group permanently—simply because the record company wanted a gospel sound. I was 18 years old and doing the one thing in life I really wanted to do—making money by singing. I felt that I had it made!

Occasionally I thought about God. "Thank you, God," I

whispered. But my prayers did not go beyond that level.

• • •

My relationship with Joyce and Telma was a little strained for a while. Yet they were professionals and knew we had to get along and work together.

I grew more self-confident after that experience. The producers liked my voice. They wanted *me* on all the background recordings and thus I began to accept myself and my ability to sing. Until the phone call, I'd been the silent member of any decision-making process. But that slowly began to change. Over the next few months, I learned to assert myself in little ways. Occasionally I made suggestions. Because I was one-third of the group, I entered into the discussions.

Then after I'd been with the group for several months, I learned we were not getting union scale from Stax. We were all members of AFTRA—American Federation of Television and Radio Artists. We had to pay dues, and had transportation costs and other expenses. The more I thought about it, the more unfair it seemed. They liked our work. They wanted us to sing. It wasn't fair for them not to pay us union scale.

Pam was home for a school break. Over the first few days we were together, I mentioned this twice to Pam, but she didn't think we could do anything about getting more money.

But I kept thinking about it. And the more I thought about it, the more disturbed I became. I don't know where I got the courage, but one day I called the treasurer of Stax. After I had explained who I was and what I wanted, I added, "This isn't fair. You're not paying us scale. I just don't think that's right."

"We've been paying each member $21 an hour all these years," he told me. "They've been doing it for that price. We're not going to pay more when they aren't asking for more."

"That's why I'm calling," I said. "I'm asking for more. We should get paid the union scale."

He was actually quite nice to me, agreeing that we deserved union scale. "Now that you've asked, we'll pay it," he said.

When I saw Pam the next day I was jazzed up with excitement about what I'd done. This would substantially increase what we got paid for each session.

But Pam wasn't happy about it. "You had no right to call and represent us," she said. "We didn't tell you to."

"Maybe not, but somebody needed to do it. And it worked, didn't it? Besides, I called them in reference to myself. Then they mentioned the others' names. We all got the raise. So they're going to pay all of us scale."*

Looking back I realize that calling the treasurer wasn't wise or tactful. I'd just turned 18, was the newest member of the group, and I had no right to take over like that.

"They might have fired us," Telma exclaimed to Pam after she heard what I'd done.

"Well, they didn't." Pam said, now trying to defend me.

I had usurped Telma's leadership. She was the leader, but I'd gone behind her back to ask for the raise. She had a right to be mad.

"Ullanda's trying to take over now that they're going to use her on all the sessions," Telma said.

"She's not trying to take over anything," Pam argued. "She felt that she needed to stand up and ask for more money for herself. And so everyone benefited. That's all there was to it!"

My actions must have made Telma feel insecure, and I didn't realize what I'd done. We might have had a lot of words if Pam hadn't acted as a buffer between us. "No, Telma, Ullanda isn't trying to do anything wrong. She's really trying to make sure we all get a fair price."

"Yeah, well, we'll see," Telma said.

Although we never discussed the incident again, our conversations were a little stiff for a few weeks afterward. Our relationship probably would have remained cool except that Telma and I started to date two men, both of whom were members of a male singing group, and we'd ride together when we went to see them.

Telma and I never got to be good friends, but we did understand each other. The relationship was a good one, and Telma was good to me. No matter what our relationship or our differ-

---

*In those days, scale was $27.50 an hour.

ences, once we got inside the studio, the professional Telma took over and she was all business. Personal issues were immaterial when we recorded. She wanted each of us to do a flawless job and to stay totally concentrated on that single goal.

A few months after the money incident, Telma and Joyce got a phone call. A new singer had emerged on the national scene named Tony Orlando. He had hit the number one spot with his song called, "Tie a Yellow Ribbon 'Round the Old Oak Tree." The two women who appeared with him in his act called themselves "Dawn."

"I've heard about you and I've listened to your work," Tony Orlando told Telma when he called. "The women who've been singing with me are leaving. I wondered if you and Joyce would like to replace them."

Tony Orlando explained that he wanted two girls who were free to travel. The original Dawn didn't want to go on the road with him, so this was a big chance for them. I knew in my heart that I would have jumped if they had invited me.

Telma and Joyce agreed to become the new Dawn. When they broke the news to me, they fairly burst with excitement. They told me about their upcoming dates and the exciting places they'd travel and perform.

Finally, unable to hold back anymore, I wailed, "You're leaving me. What will I do?"

"You'll get others to sing with you," Joyce said.

"And remember, Ullanda, it's your voice they want on all the recordings."

I thought about that. I realized that we could probably find other singers, but it would be a lot of work getting them to the standards that Telma had set.

A few minutes later, Joyce left the room and Telma came over and sat down beside me. "I'd love to have Joyce with me because we've been together a long time. But you don't think her husband is going to let her go on the road for several months at a time, do you?" (Joyce had gotten married only a few weeks earlier.)

"Probably not," I said.

"If she turns down the chance, you're next in line."

"You really mean that?"

"You know I do."

And I did. Telma didn't play games about business. Suddenly my disappointment evaporated. I was already thinking about the travel and singing on stage night after night.

But the next day, Joyce came in all smiles. She'd talked the situation over with her husband and he'd said, "No way are you turning this down."

I almost cried but I tried not to show it. I did understand. It was big money, a chance to move into the public view. Telma and Joyce would sing at Las Vegas, Los Angeles, New York, and all the big cities in Europe.

I was left out and I felt badly, but there was nothing I could do. My dreams were smashed. I'd been moving into the big time and now I felt as though everything was over.

Chapter 8

· · · · · · · · · · · · · · · · ·

The group won't die," Pam told me. "It can't."

"But I'm the only one left," I said. I didn't know how to go about forming a new group. I'd only been singing with them for less than a year and was still learning about the business. Even if I knew what to do, I couldn't have directed them the way Telma had. "I don't know how to lead a group—"

"I've been doing a lot of thinking about this," Pam said, "and I've decided to quit college and sing with the group. That will make two of us, and we'll add a third person."

At first I was shocked and wouldn't hear of her quitting school to sing with our group. But finally I realized that this is what she truly wanted to do.

"Music is my life and I'm coming back. I may not be Telma, but I know what producers want from us. Together we can do it." At that, I felt a big weight roll off my shoulders. Pam had a friend ready to audition, too, Sherrie Payne, the sister of Freda Payne, a popular Black recording artist. The three of us sounded great together and started rehearsing. Pam took care of the bookings. It wasn't long before our new group worked as much as the old one.

My life was on the upswing once again.

· · ·

"We've never met," said the woman on the other end of the line, "but my name is Jackie Hicks and I know about you and the good back-up work you do."

This call came after our new group had been together a few months. Jackie Hicks, was the leader of Motown's exclusive, female, back-up group called The Andantes. For years they'd been doing the work at Motown and backed big-time groups such as the Supremes, the Temptations, Smokey Robinson, the Four Tops, Marvin Gaye, and Tammy Terrell. Although I'd never met Jackie, back-up singers comprise a fairly small number of people. The Andantes had already distinguished themselves as *the* back-up singers in the Detroit area.

"I decided to call you because one of our girls is dropping out," Jackie said, "We need a replacement and we're looking for a soprano. So I'm wondering if you would be interested."

"I've been doing the soprano parts on most of our jobs," I said as calmly as I could.

"Yes, I know." Jackie gave me a sales pitch about the opportunities—as if she needed to sell me on the idea. "So, are you interested?" she asked.

I was elated, but I played it cool. "Yes, I think I'd be interested in meeting with you." I was just about ready to ask about when she wanted to audition.

"If you want the job, Ullanda, it's yours."

"That's it?"

"Yes," she said. "I know enough about your work already."

Suddenly it hit me that I'd reached a level of professionalism so that she didn't have to audition me. By then I couldn't hold back. "I'd love to become an Andante!" This was my first great opportunity to move ahead professionally.

But as soon as I hung up, I caught my breath—I had to tell Pam. She had dropped out of college to come back to the group. No matter what she said, I knew that part of her reason for returning was that she was my friend. She didn't want me to have to leave the business. I had a real pang of conscience about singing with The Andantes. And yet, I felt that Pam, Sherrie, and I had an unstated understanding that singing background was the prelude to the real thing. Telma and Joyce had moved on. Others in Detroit were taking whatever opportunities came their way.

"Pam," I said, when I finally got up the nerve to go over and see her, "Jackie Hicks called—"

"Yeah, I know," she said, "she got your number from me."

"They want me to take over the soprano on the Andantes."

"Yes, I know." Jackie told me. "Are you going to do it?"

"I want to," I said tentatively, trying hard to keep my excitement from showing. Seeing Pam, again I felt pain that my decision would hurt her.

"Look, Ullanda," she said briskly. "I'm glad this has worked out for you. If it will make you happy, then you ought to take it. I want the best for you," she added. "After all, you're my friend."

I grabbed her and gave her a big hug. "You're a great friend, Pam. Best I've ever had. Thank you for understanding."

So I became one of The Andantes and for several months I was able to work with both groups. I was having a wonderful time, doing the one thing I really wanted to do with my life—and getting paid for doing it. As Motown's transition intensified, however, The Andantes started to get fewer singing opportunities with the famous artists. We ended up singing more often with new artists, although we did a couple of things with the Temptations. I remember one recording in particular in which we sang background with a duet featuring Diana Ross and the Temptations. We had a few other sessions with the big-name talent, but nothing outstanding, certainly nothing like what The Andantes had been doing a year earlier. But I didn't mind. I was elated to be part of The Andantes that worked with Motown.

Then another opportunity came my way.

I had gotten along well with Jackie Hicks. We weren't close friends, but we had an enormous respect for each other. Then one day she called and said, "Ullanda, Quincy Jones just called me. He is coming to the Detroit Amphitheater for a week of live performances. He's going to be opening for Perry Como, and he wants The Andantes to do the background vocals, but I don't want to do it."

"So I wondered if you, Pam, and Sherrie would like to do it."

"Are you kidding? Hey, we'd love to take it. I know I can speak for them. This is a great opportunity. And with Quincy Jones? Are you sure you don't want to do it? What's wrong with you?"

"Oh, girl, you know I'm not into that stuff on stage with

dancing and all that. It's just not me, but I know you'd do well."

"I'd jump at the chance."

"I thought you would." Jackie laughed. "I'm going to give Quincy your number, and someone will call you. The money is great, and you're going to love it."

I was so excited, my hands were shaking when I called Pam. Pam and Sherrie were thrilled too. Two suspense-filled days later, I got a call from Quincy Jones' secretary. In short, we got the job. His people sent us the tapes to listen to so we could learn the music they wanted us to sing. If I remember correctly, each of us received $1,500 for the week, in the early 1970s, big money for back-up singers.

Whenever Quincy Jones did live performances, he appeared with a full orchestra and put on a really big concert. He scheduled us for three songs and it was easy. We would come on stage all dressed up, sing the background for the numbers, and then go backstage. That was it.

While we were in rehearsal, we got to meet Quincy Jones, who turned out to be one of the nicest men I've ever met. One night, he took the three of us to dinner. At dinner, Quincy introduced us to Toots Tillman. His name may not be nationally known, but he played harmonica with the orchestra Quincy brought to Detroit. Toots is probably the best in the business on that instrument. He's done albums and has circled the world. Hubert Laws joined us. He's a flautist, has made many albums, and more recently accompanied Kathleen Battle on "Lord, Why Come Me Here?"

Quincy Jones was funny and a fun loving person. He came across as the big-brother type and didn't try to impress us with his star status. From that gig, Quincy and I developed a friendship, staying in touch through our music until long after I moved to New York. Part of the connection was because of Patti Austin, Quincy's godchild. Later, when I was living in New York, Patti often hired me to do jingle work with her.

That's how I worked—staying open to every opportunity. Some background singers didn't want to sing except with their group. But I was different. Any kind of singing work that came my way, I went for it. Moving around and being flexible opened doors for me that I'd never otherwise see open.

Eventually, Motown completed their move to California, and most of the work stopped coming to Detroit. At that point I began to think about moving to Southern California too. If I wanted to advance in my career, I had to go where I could find the work.

In 1971, at the Stax studio, I met members of a fairly new group called The Honeycomb. Occasionally I filled in for one of their singers. The Honeycomb used me whenever they could. Sometimes I dreamed of what my life would be like if they asked me to become a permanent part of their group. About that time, I auditioned by myself for an upcoming singer named Laura Lee. She had a fine voice and a striking personality, and her gospel background came through on her records and live performances.

The opportunity to sing with Laura Lee sounded even better when she told me we'd be going on tour with Al Green, a famous pop artist. Al got booked into the best places from Vegas to the strip in Florida. A highlight for Blacks is to appear at the Apollo Theatre in New York; for going on stage there signifies acceptance and success from their own people. When I was barely 20 years old, I sang on that stage with Laura Lee. I could hardly believe it! I felt so privileged to be on that famous stage.

I've made it. I've made it as a singer. It felt wonderful inside. Such moments as these were what I lived for.

The day would come when I realized how little I settled for to make me happy.

Then one day I got a phone call.

It was the answer to my deepest dreams.

Chapter 9

. . . .

I would have to make a choice. But I didn't want to face it, so I ignored it as long as I could.

The group couldn't remain the same. Motown had moved and the amount of work available to us continued to decline. Yet while the group was doing less work, my opportunities were increasing. At times my life became a real juggling act to stay part of the group with Pam and Sherrie when I got chances to go on the road. They didn't complain, I loved singing with them, and we worked well together. But I knew that as soon as I got the chance to leave Detroit for good, I'd take it.

Then came my big chance.

And I was ready.

Laura Lee and I were booked for two weeks into a night club in Detroit called Mozombeak. One night after we finished our numbers, Edna Wright, lead singer from The Honeycomb, stopped by my dressing room to see me. Her producer-writer, Greg, was with her.

We chatted a few minutes and then Edna said, "We came to see you because we need a replacement. One of our singers has dropped out."

"We think you'd make a perfect replacement," Greg added. "If you're interested."

"Interested? Are you kidding me?" I squealed. "I'd love it."

"Just one thing," Edna said, "we don't want any problems between Laura and us. We're on the same label, so you have to settle it with her."

"Don't worry about it. When I tell her I've got this opportunity, I know she'll understand."

"We're getting ready to leave for Europe for three months. You'd have to come out to California for at least a month, maybe two, to rehearse. Can you handle that?"

"No problem. I'll be there."

As I had expected, Laura Lee took it well. She was a caring woman and understood that this kind of opportunity didn't come often. "I hate to lose you, Ullanda," she said," but it's a wonderful chance for you. You deserve it and you'd be stupid to pass it up."

My chance had come to follow my dream. *I am going to join the Honeycomb*, I told myself over and over. I would also get to live in Southern California for two months during rehearsals. Following that, we were already booked for three months in Europe.

Then it hit me—Pam. She'd stood with me all the way. I wasn't sure how she would react. I had promised to stay with the group, even though I was singing with others as well. But this time it was different. By joining the Honeycomb, I would permanently cut myself off from Pam.

I couldn't see how I could possibly walk away from the opportunity to sing with the Honeycomb, yet, my conscience troubled me. It was because of Pam that I got into the business. At last I gathered up my nerve to tell her. "Hey, that means you're going to be gone for a while," she said.

"That's right—five months or so."

"Then I think we need to replace you." Because I knew her so well, I detected the hurt and anger in her calm voice.

"I've always stood by you," she said, "and I've been your friend." She didn't say it in words, but her tone said, *I've had enough.*

But despite feeling hurt and rejected, Pam understood. She and I had been together three years and were still friends when we parted.

• • •

When I got to Los Angeles, I found another shift in the makeup of Honeycomb. A second girl had decided she didn't want to go to Europe so Edna hired Tramaine, a lovely young woman from Oakland.

Tramaine and Edna Wright were already good friends, and both were lead vocalists. The job paid good money and would be a chance for Tramaine to get more exposure as a singer. When Tramaine arrived at the rehearsals, she seemed happy. I liked her, sensing a kind, sweet person.

Tramaine lasted through the first week of rehearsals then she just quit. At the time, Edna only said, "Tramaine has decided not to go with the tour." I didn't ask why, but the abruptness of Tramaine's leaving seemed strange to me. Later I heard that Tramaine had gone to Edna and said, "I can't do this anymore. I don't like the kind of music. I don't like the kind of dancing we do when we sing. I don't like the sexy costumes we'll be wearing in front of all those people."

"I understand," was all Edna said. The person who told me added that tears filled Edna's eyes when she said goodbye to Tramaine.*

• • •

I spent the next five months on a real high. Every new European city was exciting to me. People flocked to our concerts. It seemed that every day my life grew better and better.

But unknown to me, not everything was going that smoothly.

The day after we got back to Los Angeles, Edna came to me with a shocked expression on her face. At first I wondered if someone in her family had died. For a few minutes, she was so upset she couldn't talk.

Finally she managed to speak. "Bankrupt," she said.

"What are you saying? Who's bankrupt?"

"Stax went broke while we were in Europe. They've folded.

---

*Years later I was hired to sing for the Martin Luther King Special. We were rehearsing with a choral group to accompany a well-known gospel artist—a person I knew only by name. Then a lovely woman walked into the room. Something about her looked familiar, but it took me a few minutes to figure out where I had seen her before. Then it hit me. Los Angeles, in 1973. She was Tramaine, who briefly sang with the Honeycomb. Now she's Tramaine Hawkins, from the famous gospel group, the Hawkins family, and is married to Walter Hawkins. Then I understood why Tramaine left.

No more contracts. No money. No more anything."

"Oh, no," I said. "What do we do now?"

"We try other labels, I suppose."

Edna tried other record companies, but nothing worked out and the Honeycomb disbanded. Edna and I parted and shortly after that, she left the business.*

Emotionally I fell apart for a few days. "This isn't fair! It isn't fair!" I yelled at God and at the walls of my apartment. But whether I thought it was fair or not, it had happened.

Not knowing what else to do, I made plans to return to Detroit. Totally discouraged, I did the only thing I knew that might get me work again. I called Pam and told her my sad story. She probably knew anyway, because her group had been doing background vocals for the same company. Finally I said—and it wasn't easy for me to do—"I'd like to come back to the group."

"No problem," she told me. Just like that. "The group is still here and always open to you. I'll have to talk it over with Sherrie and Janet, but I don't see any problem. I'll get back with you."

I was greatly touched and very happy. I knew I didn't deserve to be taken back. I was so thankful to have such a generous friend.

I also called Jackie Hicks. They were also willing to take me back as a member of The Andantes, even though they were also having less work. I was happy for that chance as well.

Janet Wright, however, wasn't happy that I wanted to come back to Pam's group, and I couldn't blame her for being hurt. I believe she felt I'd returned to replace her, since she had taken my place. And I remembered how I had felt when I first replaced Pam.

The first session I did with Pam and Janet wasn't fun. That was new to me, because I had loved my work and singing with the others. Janet's attitude toward me—quite naturally—was still a little edgy. I couldn't blame her. And on top of my coming back, I had taken over first soprano, which she had been doing. Singing first soprano is easier. Also, once a person's ear is trained

---

*Not until much later did I learn that Edna Wright was a Christian and the daughter of a gospel minister. She had moved out of Christian music and gone into secular success with Honeycomb. Edna married Greg, her producer, and they went back into the church. So far as I know, she no longer sings professionally.

to sing a particular part, it can be difficult to make a transition. However, after we began to work together, Janet picked up her part and did well. Our group sounded good.

But for quite a while, I didn't feel completely comfortable. Janet and Pam had become close friends, and here I was coming back. My presence certainly stressed their relationship and I felt the stress for a long time.

Then Sherrie Payne got the opportunity to sing with the Supremes and took on a full schedule with them. That left just the three of us—Pam, Janet, and me. We had a good time working together, but I gradually became aware that Pam and I had lost the closeness we'd enjoyed since high school. We were slowly drifting away from each other. I didn't know what to do about it, but I saw it happening. Maybe she knew I would leave again and just didn't want to be hurt.

Pam had been my best friend. She'd given me my first breaks in the business. Of all the people I had known and the friends I had made, none of them had been more generous and kind, so it hurt a little to realize what was happening.

· · ·

I returned to Detroit in late 1973, a bad time for the recording business. Work had dwindled since Motown's move to Los Angeles.

I didn't seem to have any opportunities to do anything except what I had been doing for three years.

Once that had been enough.

But no longer. I wanted more.

Chapter 10

. . . .

*M*y life isn't going anywhere," I said to Mom after I'd been living at home for two months. "Nothing is happening in this town any more."

After I had done a few more sessions in Detroit, I had to face the harsh reality that the work had slowed down so much it was hard to make a good living. Even those who called us didn't pay as much as they'd paid before Motown moved to California.

For weeks I had been struggling inside, trying to make a decision. I didn't want to walk away from Pam again and yet I saw no future in Detroit. I worried about this for weeks, trying to decide the best thing to do. At last I told Mom, "Unless something opens up here, I think the smart thing to do is move to southern California and try to break into the business out there."

Finally, I called several California friends and told them my predicament. "If you hear of anything I might do, let me know." They promised, but no one ever called back with good news.

I kept trying, and I refused to give up. During those weeks when I was calling everyone I knew, trying to arrange to move from Detroit, I had a surprising phone call from a high school friend, Krystal Davis. Years before she had asked me to help her get into the music business and I'd invited her to sit in on a recording session, and had introduced her to a few people. To my surprise, she told me that she was singing for Eloise Laws (a famous jazz artist) and was calling because they needed a soprano. She asked if I'd be interested.

"Am I interested!" I cried. 'I've been trying to get to

California and—"

"Just come on down. You won't even have to audition. It's a three-month engagement in Miami." As if she had to sell me on the idea, Krystal said, "It's such a wonderful opportunity. You get good money, and it's right on the Strip with the big hotels. Oh, and do you remember Renee Davis?"

"Of course I do." Renee was another high school classmate.

"I got this job because of her."

"Renee? I didn't even know she could sing."

"Honey, she got hooked up with Eloise first. And since we'd been good friends in high school, and she knew I was trying to get into the business, she got me in with Eloise." Krystal and Renee had already been in Miami for six weeks, performing with Eloise. When the new opening came, Krystal had immediately called me.

"Oh, Ullanda, you'll love it here. The three of us can live together. And wait until you see this gorgeous suite the hotel has given us!"

"I'm on my way," I said.

They sent me an airline ticket the next day.

I had only one big thing to do before I left, tell Pam about the call. In my naivety I assumed she would be as happy at this as she'd been when I had left before. Or maybe I was so caught up in my own joy that I didn't think about Pam and her reaction.

"You're going?" Pam asked and her voice was cold. "You're actually going to take this job and go to Miami for a couple of months? Then what? You want to go through all that disappointment again?"

"But Pam, I can't pass up the opportunity—"

"You left us to work with Laura Lee, and that didn't work out. You left us to go with The Honeycomb. That didn't work out. Now you're taking off for Miami. You think you can leave whenever you want? You think that when everything falls apart, you can come back and we'll say, 'Sure, honey'? If you go this time, Ullanda, you don't come back to the group."

"Pam, Detroit is dead. Nothing's happening here. I have to make money and continue to work. I have to work where the work is."

"I've stood behind you all along. But this time I don't think it's right. I don't understand why you have to leave."

"You don't understand? Think jobs. Money. No Motown. No Stax."

"We're getting enough work to get by," she said. "And they keep hiring us because we're loyal."

We talked for a long time, both knowing that this involved more than my going to Miami. We were ending a good friendship. Today, I finally understand why she felt the way she did. But back then, I felt hurt, wondering why she wanted to hold me back.

• • •

I loved my time in Miami with Krystal and Renee. All of us had strong churchgoing backgrounds and we quickly grew to be good friends. Both of them had grown up in the Baptist church and even though none of us attended now, our training had paid off, and we maintained high moral standards.

One thing struck me as odd about them. They'd both become vegetarians. "Well, it's like this," Renee had kidded me when I questioned them, "don't knock it until you've tried it. Renee and I do the cooking around here and unless you want to starve, you have to eat like us."

I didn't agree to a vegetarian lifestyle with much enthusiasm. I wondered how they could have a full meal without ever having just a little meat. To my surprise, the food was excellent.

That was 1974. I've been a vegetarian ever since.

• • •

The three of us had a great time together during the six weeks I stayed in Miami. I loved being on the Strip and going into the fancy hotels. It almost felt like Las Vegas.

I loved working with Eloise Laws, also. Physically, she was beautiful, and musically, very good. While visiting or passing through Miami, a number of famous people came to hear her sing. One night Wayne Newton walked into the nightclub. He listened and later went backstage to tell her that he heard she was in town and "just couldn't miss your act."

Listening to them talk, I thought, *This is wonderful. This is the kind of life I've always wanted. I'm finally moving up in show business. I'm around famous people all the time and everyone treats me so nicely.* And most important of all to me, I was out of Detroit and I was still working.

Of course, there were moments when I thought of home and of my grandparents. A few times my thoughts even wandered to God and the church. But not often. And, I reminded myself, I'd put my childhood religion far behind me.

I had put out of my mind something that happened as I was visiting Granddad not too long before. For as we talked I suddenly realized that he had been saddened by my decision to go into show business. "This is how my little Ullanda has gone," he said to me, disappointment filling his voice. "Child, I want the best for you." He never condemned me, but the glistening in his eyes made me realize that I'd hurt him deeply by not following God.

However, in those days I didn't have time to think about God or about disappointing Granddad. My career was moving— at last. Eloise liked me personally and appreciated my voice. She wasn't one who pushed people into the background, but liked to give others a chance. So one day she said to us, "You girls need a little exposure."

"What kind?" I asked.

"I've decided to let you girls open for me."

From then on, every once in a while the three of us became the opening act for Eloise. Occasionally I sang solos during the opening. To my amazement, I found that I enjoyed the spotlight.

It was a wonderful time.

Life could only get better!

Chapter 11

. . . .

I'll never forget the first time I sang alone in front of the Miami crowd. I was eager to do it, but I played it cool, and the questions bounced through my mind. *How am I going to pull this off? What if I get out there, sing seven words, and fall apart?* I nearly always sang soprano with a high timbre. Now I would have to use my chest voice and project. *Could I do that? Was I really good enough to pull it off?*

During our first rehearsal, I belted out the song, "Midnight Train to Georgia," a rhythm-and-blues number that calls for a gutsy, powerful, dominating kind of voice. To do it right, I had to project and grab hold of the song. To sing a high, light soprano requires much less physical energy. To sing solo, I had to get more inflection on the words and just give in to the power of the notes.

And I did it! I pulled it off, acting as if I'd been singing solos all my life. I was actually surprised how well it turned out, even as I realized I wasn't doing it quite right. When singing properly, the singer doesn't get hoarse, and I felt a rasping in my voice as I finished the rehearsal.

I was still nervous when I stood alone on the stage, the spotlights on me. But I gave it all I had and the people liked me. I felt a rapport with the audience and was thankful.

After we finished our act, Krystal turned to me with a squeal. "Ullanda, how did you *do* that? How did you learn to belt a song like that?

The strange thing was, I couldn't tell her. Somehow I knew how to do it, but I didn't know how I did it. But her approval and admiration were exactly what I needed to hear.

Maybe I ought to start moving into solo work, I thought. I still loved backup singing but my success as a soloist had given me new confidence.

When Eloise finished her six-week engagement in Miami, my work ended too. I'd hoped to get calls from friends in California, or hoped that someone would hear me and offer me work. But no calls came.

Eloise promised to keep in touch, so there was nothing else for me to do but go back home and stay with my mother. After a couple of days, I called Pam because I just wanted to see her again. But Pam was cool on the phone, and made it clear that she had no time to see me. Feeling terribly alone, I knew that I couldn't stay in Detroit without my close friends.

Then one evening at a reunion of the *Swinging Time* program gang I met a man, a singer, who introduced himself as Danny Beard. He was appearing in a musical in town and after we'd talked for half an hour, invited me to come to see the play as his guest.

I went the next night and found that Danny was one of the soloists—with an incredible tenor voice. Backstage after the show, I met some of the cast. As I watched the cast leaving the theater, my eyes fell on an attractive man. *He is so good looking,* I thought. I could hardly take my eyes off him and hoped I would get a chance to meet him. Just then a beautiful young woman walked up to him, took his arm, and they left. *Oh, well,* I thought, *he's taken.*

For the couple of weeks that Danny was in Detroit, we grew to know each other quite well. He made his home in New York and planned to return as soon as the musical group finished their national tour. Before he returned home he insisted that I should call him if I ever got to New York.

In the meantime, my savings were running low and I needed to find work. Just when I was getting to the end of my money, Eloise Laws called. "I'm opening up a two-week engagement at a nightclub in uptown Manhattan on 97th Street, at a club called Sweet Waters. Would you be available again?"

"No problem," I said. "I'll be there." Two weeks' work in New York was better than two weeks of not working in Detroit.

Once I was settled, I called Danny. "Look, I'm in town to sing with Eloise. Come to the club."

"I'll be there. Count on it."

True to his word, Danny came the first night—and every night. After the performances, he hung around and we talked. By the fourth or fifth night, we started dating. Danny took me to a couple of parties and introduced me around. One of the people I met and especially liked was Sharon Redd, who sang back-up for Bette Midler. Sharon was also doing a lot of session work for other artists.

A few days after we met, Sharon got a call to audition with a group that was going to be called Consumer Report. They'd just scored big with the major hit but, interestingly enough, a group called Consumer Report didn't actually exist.

The producers had hired professional jingle singers to do the vocals of this song for the record, releasing it under the name of "Consumer Report." To their surprise, the record became a hit. Now they were trying to figure out who they could send out on the road to perform this song and capitalize on the success of the one big hit.

Harold Wheeler who'd scored, arranged, and conducted the music tried to get the original jingle singers to go on the road. But, except for Frank Floyd, every one of them turned him down. "No way," they said. "We can stay right here in New York and make thousands of dollars singing jingles. Why should we go on the road and lose work?"

The obvious solution was to hold auditions, form a group, rehearse them quickly, and send them on the road.

At the party where we met, Sharon Redd told Danny about Consumer Report and suggested that I might be interested. Danny set up an audition for me with Harold Wheeler who hired me as soon as I finished singing. "I like your voice," he said. "And like the way you dress. You fit in well and you're the right age."

He appreciated the way I was dressed! Aunt Helen had taught me well. And I went to every audition dressed as if I were going to perform live. It usually paid off!

"We just have one problem," Wheeler said. "Frank Floyd is our male soloist, but we're still two girls short. As soon as we find

SSTUIS-3

them, we're ready to send you on the road."

"I know a couple of girls back in Detroit," I said. "Let me make some calls."

I called Pam that very afternoon, excited that we could work together again. She wasn't interested and made it very clear that she had no intention of ever singing with me again.

After her reaction I was afraid to call Janet. But I gathered up my courage and called her, explaining that they paid $500 a week.

"Ullanda, thanks, but I'm not interested."

I could understand that Pam and Janet were still hurt over my leaving. What I couldn't understand was that I was offering them a chance to move ahead in their career, but they preferred to stay in Detroit where the opportunities continued to diminish. Ten days later, Harold still needed the two female singers and couldn't find anyone suitable. So I told him I'd try my friend again.

I called Janet. "Just listen to me a minute," I said. "They still haven't found anyone. I know you're still mad at me but put aside your personal feelings for a minute and think about your career. Don't you need to work? Don't you need the money?"

"I could use the money, of course—"

Her voice had begun to soften and I realized she really did want to do it. "I just don't know," she said and I caught the hesitancy in her voice.

I explained the set-up—three months on the road, paid every week, and the likelihood that this work would bring in more.

"OK," she finally said. "I'll give it a try."

I told the producers that I had a girl. They sent her a ticket, and she came the next day. Janet auditioned, and they gave her the part. Then Janet called Pam, but she still wouldn't come.

Finally I decided to call Krystal. She'd helped me, and now I could help her. I didn't know if she was what they wanted, but she deserved the chance to show them her ability.

Krystal came to New York, auditioned, and they hired her. We went into rehearsal. We learned other songs, of course, and eventually even cut an album. We did a lot of traditionals such as "He Ain't Heavy, He's My Brother." The album sold quite well and, of course, we were excited.

I'd never met Frank Floyd, the male soloist, although I knew

that he was a popular jingle man in New York. At our first rehearsal, I gasped when I saw him. Frank was the handsome man I
had seen backstage after *The Wiz*.

It's him. It's the same man. And he's still as handsome as ever!

I could hardly take my eyes off him.

I don't know if I fell in love with Frank the man, or with
an image of the debonair, handsome man I met that day in
1975. I do know that Frank captivated me like no other man I
had ever known.

Chapter 12

• •

*I*t takes more than hard work. In the music business, people constantly talked about getting the right breaks. Many talented and creative people never seemed to get the breaks that the others talked about.

My big break in the jingle business came because I happened to be physically present when a producer needed someone. And I wouldn't have been there if it hadn't been that Frank wanted to help me. I'll always be grateful to him.

As soon as we returned to New York after our tour with Consumer Report, Frank started taking me with him to recording sessions. He'd built up an excellent reputation, and producers sought him out. When he had the chance, Frank would tell the producers that I was a back-up singer from Detroit who had sung for Motown and other artists. When he started to bring me around, they assumed that anybody he brought must be good.

One day my big break came. Patti Austin, a well-known vocalist and jingle singer, got caught in an extended session at another studio, and couldn't make it to record with Frank. After waiting an hour and a half the producer decided they were losing hundreds of dollars because of the delay.

The producer asked Frank about "that girl here with you," and Frank told him some of my background. "Ask her to sing with you on this one. Let's see how she fits in," the producer said.

I sang and they liked me.

It was that simple. I did my first session with Frank. Now I had my foot in the door.

The next day, Frank got a call from Patti, who wanted to know the name of the new girl in town who had taken her place on the session. Frank told her about me and she said that she'd like to hire me too. "I've got some sessions coming up where I could use another girl," she told him.

The jingle business in New York is set up so that every session has to have a contractor, someone to arrange for the performers. Both Frank and Patti Austin were contractors. The jingle house, or whoever hires a back-up group, calls a contractor, who then represents the group they hire. They tell the contractor they want a certain number of male and female singers, the type of music they'll sing, and other basic information such as time and place to record. The contractor then hires the other singers.

Patti got my number from Frank, called me, and asked me to do a session with her.

My career had taken off.

I began to get calls from contractors and producers.

Suddenly I was in demand.

A variety of opportunities came my way. In 1976, I did my first commercial off-camera for Coke. (That is, they did a TV spot and I did the audio portion, which means I didn't appear on the film.) In all my years as a jingle singer, I did only two commercials where I actually appeared on film. One was a wine commercial and the other was a Coke spot with Ashford and Simpson.

Singing for Coke opened the doors wide for me. The news spread, "Hey, there's a new girl in town who used to sing for Motown. She's good, and she's studying with Helen Hobbs Jordan." I loved hearing that. It was quite an honor to study with Helen Jordan because she had a reputation of working with only the best and had taught many of the top jingle singers.

I worked regularly, and the money started rolling in. Best of all, every time they aired a jingle I sang for, I got a residual check. Some checks were as small as a hundred dollars, but many of them exceeded a thousand.

Not only my career, but my romantic life had taken off. Frank was fun to be around. I liked him and our relationship grew. When we met in preparing to go on the road with Consumer Report, Frank had been dating the same girl I saw come up to him backstage in Detroit when he appeared in *The Wiz*. To my amazement, she turned out to be Phylicia Allen. (Later she married and changed her name. As Phylicia Rashad, she became a big-time TV star in the *Cosby Show*, where she played Claire, the TV wife of the character Cosby played.)

Frank and Phylicia were having differences before he started touring for Consumer Report and we began to date. We didn't tell anybody—the group, friends, or my family—because he hadn't quite gotten over Phylicia. At the same time, Frank was going through a divorce, even though he and his wife had been separated for a couple of years. Frank told me that he wanted to keep our relationship free from gossip. As I was also to learn, Frank is a very private person, so much so that I sometimes accused him of being secretive. He had great charm, but he didn't open himself up very much to anyone.

During the weeks on the road, Frank and I got to know each other better and I fell in love with him. Shortly after we returned to New York, he asked me to move in with him.

I said Yes. I suppose this decision was my last significant turning away from my grandfather's teaching. I was rather naive about it, because I assumed we'd live together until Frank got his affairs settled and then we'd get married.

The lifestyles of the people I worked with had also influenced me. Many of them were living with someone without marrying. I allowed myself to be convinced that as long as we loved one another, we weren't hurting anyone, so it was all right.

By the time I moved in with Frank, any biblical influence had been totally erased.

Or so I thought.

In my joy, I convinced myself that I was moving into a perfect world of love and domesticity. Life was wonderful, and I'd moved in with the nicest man in the world. Soon we would be husband and wife. What more could I ask for?

• • •

I was dazzled by the glamorous world Frank opened up to me. He did so much to help me get started that I became quite dependent on him, although I didn't realize it then. Although we had our differences—he smoked marijuana, for example, though he never offered it to me—it didn't occur to me to leave him. I cared about him, and I felt an immense gratitude for the way he helped me in my career.

Our relationship continued for five years. Whenever the subject of marriage came up, he made it clear that he didn't want to get married. At first I pushed, but once I realized that he had no intention of giving up marijuana, I didn't want to marry him either. I wasn't a Christian, but his lifestyle wasn't the type I wanted to be involved in permanently. On some deeper level, maybe I knew that this couldn't be a lasting relationship. But for now, it was enough.

I now had everything I had wanted in life. Or did I?

Then why did I ask myself such questions? Why did I have a sense of emptiness somewhere deep inside? Most of the time I kept myself too busy to dwell on such questions.

But the day would come when I couldn't run away from such nagging, disquieting questions.

• • •

Two or three times a year, I flew back to Detroit to see my family. I went home for Christmas of 1976 and stayed about a week. I had a wonderful time seeing everybody and being with old friends again. Too soon my vacation time ended and I had to return to New York. Mom called the house about an hour before I was to leave to catch my plane for New York. "Ullanda, before you go back, come by work and say goodbye, will you?"

"Mom, I'd love to, but I'm going to run out of time." That was true enough, but the more honest reason was that I didn't want to go to the bar where she worked and see her in that kind of surrounding.

"Please, darling, just for a few minutes."

"I'm already running late—"

"Please. Stay 10 minutes. That's all, just 10 minutes," she begged. "I'm proud of you, and I have some people here who want to meet you. Please."

Same old Mom. I was doing well, and my success filled her with pride. She wanted her friends and customers to meet her successful daughter. "OK, but it will have to be for only a few minutes."

I kept the cab waiting outside, while I hurried into the bar. As soon as Mom saw me, she grabbed me, hugged me, and thanked me for coming. Then she introduced me to a number of people. She kept hugging me and saying how proud she was of me. She paused to tell her friends and customers about the commercials I had sung and the recordings I'd done background for. Especially she enjoyed throwing out the names of the famous people I had worked with. I felt embarrassed, almost as if I were a child again with her insisting I sing in front of everyone.

Finally, I gave her a hug, kissed her, and said, "Mom, the plane won't wait."

"I love you, honey," she said.

"And I love you too, Mom," I called over my shoulder as I raced for the taxi. How was I to know that would be last time I would ever see her alive?

Chapter 13

· ·

hy did she do that? Why did she insist on my com-ing to see her at the bar? Mom had never done that before. Such strange behavior. On the flight back to New York, I kept thinking about not wanting to go to the bar to say goodbye to my mother. She actually had to beg me to do that. Later, when I thought back to the incident, I would ask myself questions. *Did Mom have some kind of premonition? Did she sense she wouldn't see me again? Was this her way of saying goodbye to me?* I had no answers. But it had been a strange experience.

At the bar, she had been extremely affectionate—again a lit-tle strange. She kept hugging and kissing me, almost as if to say, "Don't go away."

I wasn't comfortable with her doing that, and finally I'd whis-pered, "Mom, please, not in public." Mom just didn't behave that way. At the time, I passed it off as a performance for her friends and customers.

When I finally pulled myself away and headed for the door, she said, "Ullanda, give me one more hug, and I'll see you the next time you come." Again, she just didn't normally talk that way. But I hugged her, waved goodbye to the people, and hurried outside to the waiting taxi.

I got back home, to Frank's and my apartment. It was New Year's Eve 1976. Early the next morning, the phone rang. Frank, thinking it was one of our friends, picked it up and yelled, "Happy New Year!" As I sat in bed next to him, I stared at him, waiting for him to tell me who was calling. A shocked look spread across his face. "Oh, no! I can't believe this. How did it happen?"

"What is it?" Fully alert, suddenly I felt fearful. Somehow I knew the call concerned me. I waited.

"Just—just a minute." He handed me the phone.

"Hello," I said, afraid of what I might hear.

"Ullanda, it's Verbena. I've got—" she stopped and I could hear the sobs in her voice.

"What's going on?"

"Mom's dead." She burst into convulsive sobbing.

From my memory comes this picture of me with the phone to my ear and yet not hearing anything else she said. "Mom's dead." The words registered and yet I couldn't take them in. Shocked so badly that nothing got through for several seconds, I said, "What? What did you say?"

Then I knew the truth. I couldn't deny the words.

I threw the phone across the room and shrieked. "No! No! No! It can't be! It's not possible!" I began to scream. Once I started, I couldn't stop. The pain gripped me and seemed to take over. I realized I was incoherent, and yet I couldn't do anything. The screams went on.

"Calm down! Please, calm down." From far-off in the distance Frank's voice filtered through, but it didn't help.

I raced around the room, screaming and wailing. Finally exhausted and emotionally spent, I fell to the floor. Tears spilled down my face. My chest heaved, and I tried to talk, to explain to Frank, but I couldn't get the words out. In my head, I was saying, *This can't be. I just saw her yesterday. How can it be possible?*

Frank picked up the phone and said something to Verbena. Then he waited until I calmed down. When I was coherent again, he handed me the phone.

"How did it happen?" I asked.

Verbena started to tell me, pausing from time to time in a paroxysm of sobs.

As I pieced together the story, on New Year's Eve, my stepfather, William, got out his gun. A lot of people in Detroit do this New Year's Eve ritual. They go outside right at midnight, point their guns into the air, and shoot off several rounds.

A few minutes before midnight, William began to load the

gun. My mother was in the bathroom, finishing up her make-up and combing her hair. They were going out to celebrate as soon as William came back into the house.

Mom had recently bought a little puppy. Just as William finished loading the gun, the puppy raced across the room, brushed by William, who was fully concentrating on the gun. The action startled him. Inadvertently, his finger pulled the trigger. The gun went off. The bullet hit the bathroom wall, ricocheted, and struck Mom in the head. She died instantly.

My younger brother, Sheldon, was in the basement. When he heard the shot, he ran upstairs. Mother lay slumped on the floor. Blood was everywhere. William still held the gun, dazed, emotionally paralyzed, and hardly aware of what had happened.

"You killed her!" Sheldon screamed as his eyes took in the scene.

"No!" William yelled. Then he dropped the gun and rushed to my mother.

Sheldon, frightened and convinced William had murdered her, flew out of the house. He ran all the way to Verbena's house—by car a good 20-minute ride. Despite the exertion from running, he was nearly hysterical when he burst into her house.

When he calmed down enough to talk, he told her William had shot Mom. "He was still standing there with the gun in his hand."

In the meantime, William called the police to tell them that he had accidentally shot and killed my mom. The police arrived first. They called Aunt Helen to come and identify my mother's body. She and Aunt Gladys hurried over.

Aunt Gladys, filled with disbelief, wept as she viewed her sister's body.

Aunt Helen, who officially identified Mom, said, "Strange as it may seem, honey, there she was lying in a pool of blood, but she looked like a beautiful angel. Her face had a kind of smile on it, and she was very much at peace."

The police pressed charges against William because they didn't know if it was truly an accident, and took him to jail. Everyone in the family was in Detroit, trying to comfort each other. Because I had been away for several years, and I was by myself in New York, I wasn't as much involved with the family as the others. I felt totally alone. Frank was with me, but he wasn't family.

When I picked up the phone again, I still couldn't concentrate for several minutes. Verbena kept saying in a soothing voice, "Just calm down. Calm down. When you're really calmed down, call the airlines and get a flight back home as soon as you can."

"I'll get there just as soon as—"

"Ask Frank if he can come with you. You're in no condition to make the trip alone."

"OK," I said. "I'll call you back when I have a flight set up."

When I asked, Frank didn't hesitate for one second. "Of course, I'll go with you," he said. We were on our way within two hours. From the airport, a family member came and took us directly to my grandfather's house.

When Frank and I walked inside, the place was already packed with family, friends, and church members. Some of Mom's close friends had shown up. Everyone was crying.

My aunts were concerned about Sheldon too. Even today, after all these years, he still hasn't shaken off the emotional impact of seeing his mother lying in a pool of blood. Once we got past our initial outpouring of pain and grief, most of us began to admit that it may likely have been an accident. All of us knew William loved Mom. He had taken good care of us children, and had stayed with her all those years. If he hadn't loved her, he could have left hundreds of times.

Eventually, the police dropped all charges against William. Because of the angle of the ricochet, the investigators concluded that it had to have been an accident. It just wasn't possible for someone like William to shoot that accurately, they said. Even so, some members of the family would have nothing to say to William. They knew my mother was very unhappy at that time because she was drinking a lot, but they couldn't forgive him, accident or not.

I knew about Mom's drinking, of course. While home in Detroit, I also learned that she frequently called Sonja after she had a few drinks. As Sonja told me, Mom would phone and then start crying and saying things such as, "I want to die. I don't want to live. I'm praying for God to take my life. I just can't live this way anymore. I'm too unhappy."

"Mom, if you turn to Jesus Christ," Sonja would tell her,

"you can find happiness."

"No, not for me," she'd say and start crying again. "It's too late. I'm too bad even for God."

Despite any words of comfort that Sonja tried to offer, Mom couldn't believe them. "I'm too bad. I've turned too far from God."

Mom was miserable and lonely. She had been taught to follow God and knew that she had gone about as far from God as she could, and yet she wouldn't accept God's love for her. However, I like to believe she never totally got away from God. She wouldn't have been so unhappy if she had. Another strange thing I learned about Mom was that, even when she was working in the bar, she never stopped giving one-tenth of her income to God. Every week she visited Grandfather and took him her tithe.

Granddad had never given up on her. He said to me, "If she was completely bad, she wouldn't have given money to God. She got caught by sin and didn't know how to get out."

I had a hard time going through the funeral. Mom was barely 43 years old, still quite pretty, and much too young to die.

The funeral was the worst I had ever attended. All of us cried like babies as we stared at her lifeless body. Again I remembered Mom begging me to come by and see her and how reluctant I had been. Guilt flowed through me. That led to other memories of failure and turning my back on God and the church. I couldn't stop the tears.

Now Mom was gone, and I would never see her again. As the tears continued to flow, I became hysterical. I didn't want them to close the casket. Quite irrationally, I felt that as long as the casket remained open, she was still there with us. Once they closed the lid, she would be gone. Forever.

Voices tried to comfort me, but they couldn't penetrate my wall of grief. I had lost my mother, and I felt as if everything of value was gone.

Finally, I leaned over the casket and kissed her. One of my brothers pulled me away and led me to a seat. I was still crying so hard, I couldn't see where I was going.

Perhaps I would have found comfort if I had turned to prayer. But I didn't know how to talk to God.

Prayer had become a foreign language to me.

Chapter 14

· ·

I grieved over the loss of my mother. Some of it I buried, not wanting to feel the hurt. Looking back, I think I used that grief to fight even harder to do my best in the industry.

With Mother gone, I wanted to make the rest of my family proud of me. Once I got established, I had decided I would help the family by giving them whatever they needed. I wanted them to have the things they had not been able to afford before. For one thing, it meant I could help my father by sending him on a first-class vacation and enable him to enjoy life a little more. Mom's death had been especially hard on him. No matter how many years it had been since they separated, he had never stopped loving her.

I'm going to work doubly hard to try to provide for my family, I promised myself. *I'll take every job that comes along.* And jobs did come in. The extra work helped me forget. Of course, living in New York certainly made it easier for me to push away my sense of loss.

Six months passed, then a wonderful opportunity came my way. And I almost lost it.

I heard Frank answer the phone but had no idea who had called. I did hear him say, "I don't think so. I don't think she'd be interested in doing that sort of thing. No, I doubt it. Thanks for calling, but no thanks."

"Who was that and what were they asking you?"

"That was Raymond Simpson," he said. Raymond Simpson is

a singer and the brother of Valerie Simpson—she's the other half of Ashford and Simpson. "Ashford and Simpson are going on the road," Frank said. "Raymond wanted you to audition for them. They wanted you to be part of the group."

Just like that, Frank decided that I didn't want to work with them. Without consulting me at all. We'd just moved into a new Manhattan apartment—closer to our work, but more expensive— and now he took it on himself to turn down a job for me. I wanted the chance. "How could you turn it down? That would help me pay my rent." This kind of work usually paid $500 per concert.

"Sorry." He shrugged. "If you're that interested, call Raymond back." His voice made it clear that he didn't want me to make the call.

He gave me Raymond's number. "I'm definitely interested," I told him. "I'd like to audition for you." Frank didn't say anything. He just sat and listened.

I took down the address, phone number and time to meet them. That afternoon I went to their brownstone on the west side of Manhattan. I was so excited at the possibility of working with Ashford and Simpson. I'd seen them on TV and heard their records. I knew they had written many of the Motown hits I had sung for years.

Then Valerie Simpson walked in. She greeted me, then went directly to the piano and said, "Have a seat."

"I'm going to take you through some of the songs we sing to see what kind of range you have," she told me.

She began by playing, "Give Me Something Real," the song with the highest range in their repertoire. She wanted to make sure I could hit the high C's. I liked that song because it has something of a spiritual tone to it. Oddly enough, I didn't feel nervous, and I was enjoying just being with her and singing, whether or not I got the job.

About that time, Raymond, her brother, came in, sat down, and listened.

After we sang the chorus of "Give Me Something Real" twice, she nodded and got up from the piano. Valerie turned to Raymond and said, "She sounds good to me."

Raymond smiled, but didn't say a word.

I watched both their faces, waiting for her to let me know if they wanted me.

"Ullanda, if you want the job," she said, "you're hired."

"Just like that?" I smiled with joy and felt ready to dance across the room.

"Yeah, you got it." Valerie is a very serious person, but she smiled as she said the words. "Now, we've got an engagement booked for New Year's Eve." She told me the salary and added, "On top of what we're paying, we'll take care of your wardrobe." Still very businesslike, Valerie explained everything I needed to know, including when and how they rehearsed.

When I walked out of their house, I was about as happy as I had ever been in my life. This was the biggest break of my career. Anything could happen after this. Finally I'd reached the big time in my profession.

• • •

Shortly after my tour began with Ashford and Simpson, I got the Coke spot. That opportunity would never have come my way if the producers hadn't heard me singing with this first-class act.

Valerie was a songwriter and performer, but she had started out as a jingle singer even before she became half of Ashford and Simpson. Nick never really got into commercials and seems satisfied being a song writer and performer. Valerie still does commercials. She sang "Gentlemen prefer Hanes," which is probably her best-remembered jingle. The one I think of and especially liked was, "Double your pleasure, double your fun," which she did for Double Mint gum. That ad ran for at least 10 years.

Valerie and Patti Austin were truly the queens of the jingles and already well established in the business when I got to sing a jingle with them. On the day that happened, I felt I had really arrived. Everything was going just about perfect. If there was a down side, it was that I had to work at being sociable and fitting in with the music scene. Even though I never considered myself a Christian, the people I worked and associated with lived differently from the way I had been brought up. Although good people, most of them were into social drinking and partying—the kind of things I had been protected from as a child and young teen.

"If you're going to make it," Frank said more than once, "you need to know the right people. You meet the right people by accepting invitations to parties. Don't just go and stand off by yourself. Put a little effort into getting to know them. Smile and be nice. They'll remember and call you when work comes along."

I learned to loosen up a little because I was serious about my work. To move ahead and succeed meant I had to learn not to be standoffish. That wasn't easy for me, but I did learn to mix fairly well. I attended the parties and other functions, and I don't think it showed that I never felt totally at ease.

Frank was right. My loosening up did help my career. But I never liked that part about the business. He frequently reminded me, "Who you know and who knows you are more important than your talent. Just don't ever forget that." I hated to hear that. I tried to stay out of the political game by being friendly to everybody. I developed friendships among those who couldn't help me climb upward. No matter how the business worked, I wanted to enjoy the good life I had found.

Really, I admitted to myself, *going to a few social functions is such a small price to pay for what I've gotten out of it.*

"Life just can't be much better," I said to myself and to my friends.

It really wasn't that good, but I kept trying to convince myself that I now had everything. If this wasn't everything I wanted, then what was there?

I didn't like those dark thoughts.

Chapter 15

. . . .

*I*f only Frank and I could get along better. If only he would change.

I felt that it was this one little thing that marred my total happiness. We just weren't as compatible as we ought to be. From the beginning, we'd had our differences. I assumed he would change. But he didn't. Frank was Frank, and he stayed who he was. Slowly our relationship untangled. Conflicts arose that didn't get settled so easily. In 1979, after five years of being together, vacation plans proved to be the issue that finally broke us up.

We usually took our vacations together, going to Jamaica or one of the Caribbean Islands. I enjoyed planning ahead, getting as much fun out of the planning as I did the vacation. With Frank, it was the other way around. He couldn't make up his mind for weeks, sometimes months. Then he'd announce, "Hey, let's go to the islands."

He'd announce this just days before the holiday, always at times when it was too late to get good rates or accommodations.

In July of 1979, I decided to plan our Christmas vacation. Not only would I enjoy arranging every detail, but wouldn't have to scurry around trying to get plane or hotel reservations at the last minute.

"I'm going to start now, six months in advance," I announced. "We'll know where we want to go, what we want to do, and can have our pick of hotels—the whole bit. OK with you?"

"Sure, fine," he said. "Sounds like a good idea."

So I planned the trip. It took numerous phone calls and visits to my travel agency, but at last it was finished. Our dream vacation in Jamaica. Then Frank and I had an argument. In the middle of it, he announced that he wasn't going.

Reluctantly, I canceled the trip and decided to go to Detroit. Then I started shopping. It took days for me to find the perfect gift for every family member and friend that I'd be with at Christmas. I chose things that I felt everyone would treasure. Shopping helped ease the hurt I felt over Frank's attitude.

For the first time in our five-year relationship, I wondered if he used the Christmas vacation as a way to keep me in line, to make me do the things he wanted to do and to vent his frustration because of my singing on the road with Ashford and Simpson.

Three weeks before I was ready to go home, Frank said, "I've changed my mind. I want to go with you to the Caribbean."

I couldn't believe him! I told him it was impossible. I explained that I'd bought expensive gifts for my family and friends. But he sounded so very sorry. I gave in.

"I'll call the travel people," I told him, "but if you change your mind again, that's it. I'll go home."

That seems a simple enough declaration, but I don't know where I got the courage to stand up to him. I'd never stood up to him before. But this time I told him, "This is it! If you change your mind again, it will be too late."

"I won't change my mind."

Feeling humiliated, I called my travel agent again. She couldn't get us into the best hotel. We would have to pay top rates for both airfare and hotel. But I swallowed my pride and did it.

Then I went back to the jewelry store and asked to return all the gifts I'd bought. It was terrible. The manager reminded me that they'd spent untold hours with me, helping me choose the perfect presents. But they took the gifts back and returned my money. I'd send the money home instead of gifts.

Exactly one week before Christmas, we had another argument. It was over Frank's younger brother, Bobby. He came for a visit and Frank got jealous. This happened every time Bobby came. As soon as he went back to Chicago, Frank did it again. He started an argument, and as words flew back and forth he gave me his punch line: "I'm not going."

I didn't even ask what he meant. Maybe I'd known all along that it would end this way.

"All right, that's fine," I said, surprised at the calmness in my voice. "I may as well go to Detroit."

"Do whatever you want."

"Frank, if you do this, I'm going home and when I come back I'm going to start looking for my own apartment. I'll never come back to you again."

"Oh, you'll be back," he said with a laugh.

It was four days before Christmas.

Somehow I made it through the next four days. I had to stay in the apartment, as I had no where else to go. All I could think of was getting home with my family.

The day after I arrived Frank called. "Have a good flight?"

"I'm not coming back," I said and hung up.

He called again. Several times. Each time he'd ask, "When are you coming back?"

I kept my voice cold. "I'm not coming back. Believe those words."

He didn't like my attitude or what I said. And I don't know. He had such a hold on me that maybe I would have gone back, except that I met Norman.

I'd known Norman for years. We had dated a few times when I still lived in Detroit. Meeting him during that Christmas vacation canceled Frank out of my personal life.

I hadn't seen Norman since I was in high school, but he hadn't changed that much. He was tall and still good-looking. We'd dated back then, and people said of Norman, "He's a young man with a future."

Norman graduated from high school, left for college, and I never saw him again. Through mutual friends, I'd heard that he had never married, that he lived in California, and was very successful in business. No one ever was clear on what type of business he was in.

"I'm just home for the holiday," I told him when we met. We'd run into each other in a Detroit night club. It felt great to see him, but emotionally I winced. I was still filled with sorrow and regret because Frank wasn't with me and because I didn't have a home any more in New York. For now, however, I pushed aside those concerns and asked Norman to sit down at my table.

"Only for a minute," he said. He nodded toward a table of people he'd come with. I was delighted to see him again. The timing was perfect. I knew I couldn't live with Frank any longer and felt sad and just a bit lonely. You don't put an end to five years of your life without some sorrow.

Norman didn't stay at my table for long, but he wrote down my phone number. The next day he called and asked me to go out with him. We spent most of my free time together, until I returned to New York.

Within a week after returning to New York, I found an apartment—a beautiful place on the east side of Manhattan. It wasn't cheap, but the rent was within the range I could afford. Just one thing worried me. Would work continue to come in? People knew and liked Frank. With our being split up, would they still call me? I spent several restless nights worrying about my future.

Despite my concern about money, I went ahead with the move. Immediately I started to take my things out of Frank's apartment. Once, during a particularly violent argument, Frank had hit me. Separated from him, I was afraid he might get violent, so I decided I wouldn't go to his apartment unless someone else went with me.

A girlfriend helped me move my personal things out, and I hired movers to pick up my furniture. The last time I went to his apartment, I was alone because I hadn't expected him to be home. He came in minutes after I arrived.

"Why are you doing this to me?" he asked. "I thought you cared."

"I did care, Frank," I said.

"But you're leaving. If you cared, you'd stay."

"We've been through all this. I have had it. For five years you've done the same things over and over. You're still using marijuana. You're jealous. I can't depend on you to stick with anything you promise. I'm sick of the whole thing."

"Please, give me another chance."

"Not this time," I said. "There's no way I'm going to stay, no way I'm coming back into this relationship. It's over." Tears filled my eyes as I spoke because I still cared about him. But I knew I was doing the right thing.

For a few days I kept myself too busy to think about Frank. Once I settled in, I expected loneliness to overwhelm me but to my surprise, I wasn't lonely. Also to my surprise, I didn't feel grief about leaving Frank. I think I knew our relationship was over, long before I admitted it to myself. Had I been more assertive, I probably would have left at least a year earlier.

Friends helped make the transition easier. They called, came to see me, and invited me to do things with them. Just as surprising, calls for sessions continued to come in.

For a few weeks after my move, Frank called every few days. Once he asked me to come back home. Another time he came by my new apartment, on the pretext of seeing my new place. Again, he tried to reconcile. "I could move in with you," he said. "It would be good like it was before."

But after several weeks Frank realized that it was over. Although we kept a professional relationship and continued to record together, he stopped calling me.

Outwardly, both of us were doing fine.

I wasn't doing as well as I appeared to everybody. Something in my life was missing, but I still didn't know what. I didn't like to think about any missing pieces in my life, but sometime I had to stop running. I wished then that I was a little girl again, back in Detroit, with Granddad nearby to talk to me and guide me.

My other big concern at that time revolved around one question—will I be able to pay my bills? I was paying four times as much rent as before and I didn't know if I could manage. But no matter how troubled I felt about my situation, I remained determined to succeed on my own, without Frank.

I was nearly 29 years old.

I had survived this far on my own.

I would make it.

• • •

"Hi," a man's voice said when I answered the phone. "I told you it wasn't goodbye."

"Norman!" I squealed. "Oh, I'm so glad you called. I really

enjoyed seeing you again in Detroit."

"I haven't been able to forget you," he said.

That phone call came only a few days after I returned to New York, and it was the beginning of a new phase of my life. A couple of weeks after I got settled in my new place, Norman flew in from California and spent several days with me. Then I flew out to see him.

Because we'd dated years earlier, it was easy to feel a bond with the sweet fun-loving guy I'd know in high school. His attention helped me get over Frank, and I began to believe that true happiness was just within my reach. Although we didn't see each other in person more than six or seven times, by the end of January 1980—a month after we had met again in Detroit—we started to talk about marriage.

I know we rushed into this. Part of it may have been that I subconsciously felt I had to have a man in my life. Maybe I was too dependent, too insecure to face life alone. Part of it had to do with high school memories. Back then I'd been impressed with the type of person he was. He had changed, of course, but I still related to the 18-year-old Norman. Maybe in his mind, I was still a teenager too. When Norman asked me to marry him, I didn't hesitate.

My emotions were totally caught up in this rush; every romantic instinct told me this had to be right. Tall, handsome, intelligent, knowledgeable, well-educated, and successful, Norman was also thoughtful of me. Every day or two I'd get a letter, a card, or a small gift from him. He phoned almost every night. Sometimes he'd only talk a few minutes, then say something like, "I'm going to the store, and I'll be out a couple of hours. Just thought I'd tell you that in case you called."

No man had ever been so attentive and thoughtful before. I loved it.

On Valentine's Day, February 14, 1980, we were married in a private ceremony. On March 21—five weeks later—I told Norman of my plans to divorce him.

Before the end of the first week of marriage, I knew I'd made a terrible mistake. I had not married the real Norman, but the Norman of my fantasies. He had big problems that I knew nothing about. However, I respect his privacy enough not to write about them. I can say only that we should never have married. If we hadn't rushed into it, eventually both of us would have realized how incompatible we were.

Why did I agree to marry him? Perhaps I just wanted to get married and live a normal life. Maybe I wanted to believe in fairy tales and I needed him to be my prince charming. Maybe I just needed a replacement for Frank, and missed him more than I was willing to admit to myself.

Whatever the reason, Norman and I had gotten married, and it had been a mistake for both of us. Norman wanted our marriage to work, and asked me to stay with it. But I couldn't. "No," I said firmly. "It isn't working now, and it won't work no matter how long we stay together. We're walking in different directions."

He admitted that was true. We came from quite dissimilar backgrounds with different values. I retained an attorney and learned that it was too late for an annulment. I would have to go through a divorce. I felt guilty and ashamed, but I had made the decision to marry. I had made the decision to leave. I could learn to live with my mistakes, but I did hurt inside.

Despite my background in the church, I didn't pray during that ordeal. I had turned so far from everything I had learned that I felt sure God wasn't interested in hearing me.

Only a few weeks after I thought I'd found lifelong happiness, I felt more alone than I ever had in my life.

By contrast, my career continued to move along. Some of the top people in the business asked me to sing. More money came in than I'd ever dreamed possible. Yet the money and the fame did nothing to take away the emptiness inside.

"One failed long-term relationship with Frank. One failed short-term marriage with Norman," I remember crying out. "Will I always be a failure with men?

Then life took an upturn.

I began to hope once again.

Chapter 16

· ·

*I*t started with a stare and a hello," I told my friends later. It really did begin just that simply.

I first met Tyrone in the summer of 1981. I was attending a party by myself at Rockerfeller Plaza. I was hot and thirsty, so decided to walk over to the wet bar and get myself a glass of juice. By then, I had "worked" the room and had grown just a little tired of smiling at people.

Just then I passed an extremely good looking man, going in the opposite direction. He paused and stared, then smiled at me as though we knew each other. After my terrible situation with Frank and then Norman, I'd dated other men, but each time broke it off. My relationships with men had left me angry and frustrated, and I had purposefully come alone to the party.

A few minutes later he found a way to speak to me. He told me that he was a model, and worked for the Zoli Agency. He had a nice, easy-going manner and it felt good just to chat, without getting seriously involved in the conversation.

Two weeks later, I attended another party, this time I was with a man named Nathan. We'd dated for nine months, but when Nathan started getting serious, I broke it off. A few weeks before our breakup, we'd accepted invitations to attend a rather special party—one that I felt I needed to attend. So we kept the date, understanding that it was our last.

To my surprise, shortly after we arrived someone came up behind me. It was Tyrone. We talked a while and I finally gave him my phone number.

He called the next day.

We talked. We laughed. We arranged to meet. After that Tyrone and I saw each other every day. He lived on the west side, and my apartment was on the east side. Within three weeks, we were going back and forth to one another's apartment and spending all of our free time together.

Something marvelous happened during that short period of time. I grew to love Tyrone—something I hadn't thought I could do again so easily or so soon.

Frankly, it surprised me that Tyrone wanted to date me. His picture appeared in a number of ads, and this made him a very sought-after man. Tall and muscular, his color is what I call Portuguese black. Besides his good looks, Tyrone is bright and very charming.

I had not been looking for a relationship and then, suddenly, I was in one. We became the talk of the town among the people we both knew. At the time we met, he had been casually dating four other women, but he broke up with each of them. When they saw that he'd gotten serious about me, they were shocked. "That man just doesn't get serious about any woman," one of them told me.

Six weeks after Tyrone and I began dating, I opened for a popular singer named Peabo Bryson, at one of the newest and hottest night clubs in New York. I arranged for my whole family to come to New York and stay with me in my apartment. When they arrived, I was busy doing a session, but I left them a key and told them to go on inside.

When I got home, Aunt Helen ran to meet me, about as excited as I'd ever seen her. "Ullanda! You didn't tell me who you were dating."

"Yes I did."

"No. I mean, you didn't tell me *who* you were dating. You didn't tell me he was a model." Well, Aunt Helen just raved on about him. She'd actually cut his picture out of GQ and kept it in a drawer for more than a year. "I can't wait to meet him," she told me. "Can I meet him?"

Having Aunt Helen excited about meeting him set the family up to like Tyrone. And they did like him—at least in the beginning. They were delighted that he and I had become in-volved.

But an awkward situation arose during their visit, one that became an ongoing problem—having to choose between him and my family. They'd come to New York to see me, but he wanted me to stay with him. It seemed so easy to him. "They can stay at your place," he told me.

"I—I don't know," I mumbled. His statement pushed me into a dilemma. I wanted to please him—I surely didn't want to break up with him—but I didn't want to hurt my family. They wouldn't understand. I had no idea how I was going to handle it.

When Tyrone got ready to go back to his apartment that evening, he took my hand and said to them, "Ullanda will see you guys tomorrow."

"You're going with him? And leaving us here?" asked Aunt Helen.

"What's wrong with you, girl?" my brother Carlos asked. "We're family, and we came all the way from Detroit to see you. Now you're going to stay at his place?"

"Yeah, I guess so."

"We came all the way from Detroit just to be with you. And you can't stay here with us?"

"No, she's going with me," Tyrone spoke up. "You can see her later."

I don't remember how I tried to explain it to the family, but I did exactly what Tyrone wanted. As foolish as it sounds now, I convinced myself that they'd be going back to Detroit in a few days and after they left, I still wanted to be with Tyrone. I was afraid of losing him. It's that simple. Now I was afraid Tyrone would leave me. I was still so vulnerable in my relationships with men, and I didn't want anything to jeopardize what Tyrone and I had developed.

● ● ●

Tyrone formed a mail-order business called TySpears Cosmetics, a skin care company for men. By providing the needed funds to help him get started, I became part owner. We decided to put the company office downstairs in my apartment because it had its own entrance. We closed off the upstairs to make it private. When clients came, he could go downstairs and work with them.

Sometimes when Tyrone couldn't be in the office, I stayed there and answered the phone. He advertised almost exclusively in GQ magazine and used his own picture. The ad listed a number to call to buy the products. He got calls for the cosmetics, but he got more than that. He had constant phone calls from women who were trying to figure out ways to meet Tyrone Spears.

"This is ridiculous," I said to him several times. "I didn't know women were that way."

Tyrone shrugged and laughed because he was used to it. "That's how people are." I talked to him about this many times, but he said there was nothing he could do about these women calling. "Ullanda, that's how I have to do business."

His actions told me that he loved me, but I had a hard time with the women—all kinds of women—trying to seek him out. He stayed loyal to me, too. Both Tyrone and I wanted someone to love us for who we were and not for looks, talent, or money. We felt we'd found that in each other.

• • •

"What more could I expect in life?" I wondered why the questions were starting to haunt me again. Didn't I have everything going for me? To assure myself, I thought of my beautiful apartment on New York's East 65th Street. My closet was not only filled with beautiful clothes, but I owned four gorgeous fur coats, and my friends envied them. All of them commented on my jewelry.

And money? Even as a kid growing up in Detroit, I couldn't have believed that money would come in so fast and so easy. I was singing—doing the one thing I wanted most to do in life—and all these other things were there as well.

Yes, it was the good life.

Everything was going so well.

Almost everything, I admitted. My relationship with Tyrone was dragging me down. And I didn't even understand why.

I knew our relationship wasn't right, but I didn't understand it. All my friends told me that I was leading a charmed life. I was supposed to be happy.

So what was wrong with me?

Chapter 17

. . . .

I trusted Tyrone.

Yet aggressive women constantly chased him. Most of their attempts I could laugh at. The one that I didn't laugh at involved Debbie Allen and her sister, Phylicia.

Debbie Allen became a star because of her dancing and choreography for the TV series, *Fame*. She dated and later married Tyrone's best friend, Norman Nixon, who was then a basketball star for the L.A. Lakers. One night, I took Tyrone backstage to introduce him to Debbie's sister, Phylicia, who was appearing on Broadway in the musical hit, *Dream Girls*.*

A few months later, I had to go out of town. While I was gone, I learned that Debbie had tried to bring Phylicia and Tyrone together. Because Tyrone said no, nothing more came of it. I was shocked that Debbie would try to do such a thing. She had to know that not only were Tyrone and I involved, but we were living together.

I'd considered Phylicia my friend. I had met the Allen sisters during the early days when I started to sing with Ashford and Simpson and admired Phylicia as a beautiful, talented, well-educated and genuinely nice person. This wasn't the kind of behavior I would have expected from her. If Tyrone had succumbed to her or actually dated her, I would have felt betrayed by both of them. Not only did Tyrone say no, but he himself told me about

---

*She was still single and called Phylicia Allen. After her marriage, of course, she became known as Phylicia Rashad.

what she had done long before I heard it from friends.

It would have been bad enough if it had happened once, but it didn't stop there. Phylicia tried a number of approaches such as inviting him to come to the Cosby show tapings. He didn't go.

Sometimes one or the other of them called, inviting Tyrone to meet them or go somewhere with them. But they wouldn't mention that Phylicia would be with them. This happened over and over again.

"You know, they did it to me again," I can still hear the disgust in Tyrone's voice. "They invited me out and then I learned they had Phylicia with them." After the four of them had gone out together several times, Phylicia started calling the office for Tyrone. Usually she said she had called to invite him to a session. Without me.

At first I didn't know how to react, and it took me a while to calm down. Once I got past my initial anger, I decided not to do anything. Tyrone had volunteered the information about her calls. I trusted him.

Phylicia was only one in a line of female callers. Many women—some of them well known—phoned or left messages for him. But Tyrone was loyal. I respected him because he didn't allow his good looks to cause him to stumble. He realized that certain women liked him because he was handsome. More than once he referred to a celebrity who called frequently and wanted to go out with him. He didn't return her calls because, as he said, "She doesn't have any interest in me as a person."

Tyrone's faithfulness naturally made me think about marriage. We were in a committed relationship. Marriage seemed the next step. And, deep inside, I never completely got past the sense of guilt over our living together. I often thought that I had let down my family by living openly with Tyrone. In the beginning, I knew marriage would have to wait. For the first six months after we formed TySpears Cosmetics, I put in a lot of hours working for the company. On top of that, I invested heavily to get it off the ground. Soon the company was doing well and TySpears Cosmetics started to make profit. Now that the company was earning money, I brought up the subject of marriage.

"Tyrone, why don't we get married?" I asked. By then we had

been together two years.

"One of these days, but not now. I'm not ready yet."

I was getting impatient. No matter how much I had changed, I believed in marriage. I had gotten involved with Frank and later Tyrone with the underlying assumption that this was the prelude to marriage.

"Let's just think about it for a few months," he said. "Eventually I'll marry you, but not now."

"All right," I said. I wanted to believe him.

Another year went by. My career continued to swing upward, and I was making a lot of money. We had everything we wanted. My family, however, pressured me to get married or leave. They felt Tyrone had taken advantage of me, and remained convinced he was using me by holding on without a commitment. That way I would continue putting money into TySpears Cosmetics. Actually, plenty of money came in and sales increased, but Tyrone put most of it into advertising. For instance, it cost him $16,000 to keep a monthly ad in GQ magazine.

It was bad enough that my family knew I was sinking money into TySpears Cosmetics, they also heard rumors that he was fooling around with other women. This wasn't true, but they believed what they heard.

Finally, out of deep concern, Aunt Helen phoned me and talked at length about my relationship with Tyrone. "Ullanda, if you are happy with him, we have no business interfering with your life. If he's not right for you, then you have to decide that, not us. We're your family. We'll stick by you."

"I care about him. He says we'll get married."

"Well, maybe. Maybe not. Anyway, you have to decide. It's your life."

As I listened to her, I reflected on my relationship with Tyrone. I wasn't particularly happy. Although I couldn't have said it then, Tyrone was not the problem. I wasn't happy about my life. The more I looked at our relationship, the more disappointed and hurt I felt that we hadn't married and that he wasn't interested in getting married.

"I'll think about it," I told Aunt Helen.

I did think about the situation. Often.

"We have to spend more time together if our relationship is going to survive," I finally said one night. "You're out with your friends so much. It may be business or not, but our relationship is suffering."

"Yeah, you're right," he admitted. Yet he always seemed to have an excuse ready when he wanted to go out with his friends and stay out until dawn. On top of all this, he made it clear that he still didn't want to get married. During this period, I traveled with Ashford and Simpson most weekends, gone nearly four months out of the year. When I came back to New York, I wanted to spend as much time with Tyrone as I could.

Then all of a sudden I was tired. I had no energy.

So I went to see a doctor. He found nothing wrong with me—except a fibroid tumor that he said I shouldn't worry about. So I put it out of my mind. Within a year, however, the tumor had grown to the size of a grapefruit and I began to worry. I had to do something. I was sick and tired of feeling sick and tired. I wanted my old energy back. I wanted to feel healthy again.

The doctor warned that in removing the tumor he might have to take out my uterus, too. "Do you understand what that means?" he asked me. "You won't be able to have children. How do you feel about that?"

"I'm not getting married anyway, so it doesn't really matter." I was in such a low state that I couldn't think or feel anything positive. My relationship with Tyrone had continued to deteriorate. Daily I fought depression. I just wanted to be my old self again.

"You're sure?"

"I don't have to have kids," I said. "In fact, I don't care about having children."

Satisfied with my answer, he started to talk about surgery. In the meantime, I looked into alternate kinds of treatment. Nothing helped. And so I agreed to surgery.

As it turned out, the doctor did have to remove my uterus. At that time I didn't give much thought to the implications of not being able to have children. That's something I learned to regret.

Chapter 18

I faced surgery alone.

My family would have come, but I insisted that they wait.

I'd assumed Tyrone would be with me, but he wasn't. He didn't come to the hospital and his absence hurt me deeply. Before going into surgery, I kept thinking, *Here I am, in the hospital getting ready to be cut on for major surgery, and he doesn't come to visit me. Yet he's my business partner, the man I live with, and the man I've been wanting to marry.*

The surgery went well. Through a fog of anesthesia, I heard the doctor say, "Everything looks fine."

The next day Tyrone walked into my room with a smile on his face and leaned over to kiss me. "Why didn't you come yesterday?" I asked, pushing him away. "I needed you here then."

"Sorry, but I had so much going at the office. And you know, it's so far away. It takes two hours to get here. But it's all right, I'm here now."

I turned my face away and silently cried.

• • •

After I got out of the hospital, my sister Sonja and my Aunt Gladys came to stay with me for a week. They volunteered to care for me until I was feeling healthy again. Tyrone was around, but he went out more than he stayed at home. Of course, Tyrone knew my family didn't like him, so that probably had a lot to do with it.

The night before Sonja and Aunt Gladys were to leave, Sonja and I sat down together and had a long, sister-to-sister talk. Or at least it started that way. I told her how much I would miss her and how much it meant to me for her to be there.

"Things haven't been going right for you these days, have they?" she asked gently.

"You know the answer to that."

"Maybe it's time for you to think about Jesus Christ. Maybe it's time to make a change in your life."

I can't remember what I said, but I let her know I had no interest in talking about God. Mostly, though, I just listened.

"You've had much success. You make a lot of money and live in a nice apartment," she said. "You've got diamonds, furs, and a new Mercedes. You have everything you've wanted, right? But you're still not happy. You're living with a man you aren't married to, and that's not bringing you any happiness."

Her words hit home, but I didn't like hearing them.

"It's time to make a change, Ullanda. When are you going to give your life to the Lord?"

I didn't feel she was condemning me, only pleading for me to surrender, but I said, "You can't expect me to give up all this and follow the Lord. I've worked too hard and too long to make it in the business and—"

"What if you die in sin and don't have an opportunity to give your life to the Lord? Then you'll be lost eternally. Then what value are the diamonds and your Mercedes?"

"Sonja, please pray that if anything ever happens to me, or if my life is ever threatened, that I'll have time to give my life to the Lord before I die." By then I was feeling extremely uncomfortable and didn't want to keep the conversation going. "If that happens, I'll repent, and everything will be fine. We'll be in heaven together. So don't worry about it."

"I do worry about it. Ullanda. I worry about you. Salvation doesn't work that way. You have to prepare yourself. You have to learn about who Christ is, and changes have to take place. You were brought up in the church, so you know better. Why are you continuing to live in sin like this?"

"Look, Sonja, I'm not ready. I don't want to give my life to

God, and I don't want to hear any more. If you really care, then pray for me and maybe things will work out."

I wasn't ready to change. Not yet anyway. But maybe some-day . . .

After Sonja and Aunt Gladys left, I was still weak and unable to go anywhere. I could take care of myself, but I couldn't sing or do jingles. Besides that, Ashford and Simpson were about to go back out again, and they were wondering if I would be well enough to take the next trip.

"Just be patient with me," I kept reassuring them. "I'm trying to get well as quickly as I can." I took life easy, rested often, and didn't overextend myself. Fortunately, by the time they were ready to start on the road—a month later—I was feeling all right. Not great, but I was able to start rehearsals. Once re-hearsals were over, we flew to California to start the tour, do some sessions for Motown, and sing for Smokey Robinson on TV. Each day I grew a little stronger.

After we did the first segment of the TV taping, we had a few days off. I'd gotten a call to do a jingle session in New York. *Instead of staying in California*, I thought, *why not make some money?* I decided to fly back to New York, do the jingles and be back in California by the time they were ready to do more taping.

I booked a seat on what they called the red-eye flight, a plane that leaves just after midnight and arrives at New York the next morning. Something happened on that flight that changed my life.

● ● ●

During the night, we hit heavy turbulence. In my terror, the plane seemed like a kite being tossed up and down in the atmos-phere and all over the sky.

The pilot may have been in control, but as far as I was con-cerned, we were at the mercy of the storm. I held back my screams, but I was frightened. And I wasn't the only one. Flight attendants awakened everybody. "Please be alert. We're going through heavy turbulence. Please make sure your seat is in the upright position and your seatbelts are securely fastened." They walked briskly up and down the aisle, making sure everyone had complied.

As the rumble of thunder shook our plane, and flashes of lightening continually lit up the dark sky, I was struck by a terrible thought. *I could die in this plane, and that would be the end of my life. What if that's how it ends? What am I going to do?*

Then I remembered Sonja's words. In my mind, I could hear her say, "You made a promise to God. Isn't this a life-threatening situation? Now what?"

No matter how much I tried to ignore the storm or push Sonja out of my thoughts, I couldn't do either. And I couldn't rise above my fear. "If my life is ever threatened . . ." I'd said those words, and now they were taunting me.

I tried to reassure myself that I wasn't in a life-threatening situation. But the fear was too strong. *What do I do now?*

Something inside me—not an audible voice—kept whispering, "Just surrender, Ullanda. Just surrender."

Oh, no, that's not fair. Not now. I can't become a Christian yet. It's only been a month since I made that promise. God, you have to give me more time.

From deep inside, I heard that voice again. "Ullanda, your life *is* threatened. You need to make a decision now to serve Me. You may die on this plane. You don't know what's going to happen."

But I can't! Not yet!

I have no idea how long this went on, probably only two or three minutes. I didn't want to surrender, but I felt I wouldn't leave that plane alive if I didn't. The plane bounced even more furiously as I argued with the words that kept coming to me. Finally I couldn't hold out any longer.

OK, God, I'm ready, my heart cried. *Forgive me for all my sins. Save me from a plane crash. If you spare my life, I will do whatever you want me to do.*

As I prayed, a sense of peace slowly came over me, even though the storm did not abate. My hands relaxed. I knew it was going to be all right. I sat in the semi-darkness of the plane, knowing we would not crash. Within five minutes, the plane leveled off, and we left the turbulence behind.

I was so relaxed that I sank into a comfortable sleep. One of my last conscious thoughts was, *This prayer thing really works.*

God heard me. Everything is fine, and I'm at peace.

In New York, I got off the plane and went to my sessions. Outwardly nothing had changed. Yet I felt different.

• • •

The recording sessions went smoothly. Then I got ready to go back to California for more TV programs with Ashford and Simpson and with Smokey Robinson. During the four days I spent in New York, I had forgotten about God and my promise.

After all, when people are scared, they do strange things, don't they?

Chapter 19

. . . .

One way to avoid God is not to think about serious issues or problems. That's how I handled what had happened to me on the plane. Clearly, I'd had an experience of some kind, but it had not impacted my life significantly. I didn't let it.

Landing in California, I immediately checked into a hotel and turned on the TV to watch while I unpacked. The channel had been set to a religious program but I quickly changed channels. I didn't want to be reminded of my experience on the plane. But nothing interested me and when I flipped back to the *700 Club*, a young man was singing, and I liked his voice. I decided I might as well leave it there while I unpacked.

Then the man sat down beside the host and began to talk. He said he had been fairly successful as a pop singer. Now he was a Christian artist. "I'm happy in the Lord," he told his audience. "Today I love to sing for Jesus Christ." He began to tell the audience about the changes in his life. "There was a time when I used to think that if I had money, the latest sports car, a beautiful home, and all the things that money could buy, I would be happy. Now I know that happiness comes only through Jesus Christ."

Suddenly my attention was riveted as if he were speaking only to me. Even though the skeptical part of me was saying, *Oh, sure, I've heard all that before,* another part of me listened intently. Later in the program, when the host extended an invitation to sinners who wanted to turn to Jesus Christ, I almost laughed out loud. *Why would anyone want to do that?*

Then I heard myself softly say, "I wish I could give in to God that easily."

I couldn't believe I'd spoken. And yet as the words came out, I knew they were true.

I dropped on the bed, unable to finish unpacking. Then the quiet voice I had heard on the plane spoke to me again. The words were so clear I couldn't deny them: "Ullanda, you *are* a born-again Christian. I heard you on the plane, and I accepted you. Now I want you to surrender your life to me and work full time in My ministry."

"This can't be real! What's happening to me?" I said aloud.

I'm not one of those people who hear voices—especially God's voice—speaking. Yet something inside my own head spoke so powerfully I couldn't ignore or deny it.

Accepted me? How could I be a Christian?

"God," I called out, "I don't want to be a Christian!"

Then I heard myself ask, "Or do I?"

Just that suddenly I realized that God had heard my prayer on the plane. Like it or not, now I belonged to God. I had made a promise to Sonja—even though I was only half serious—and God had honored that promise.

"I am a Christian," I said aloud. "I am a born-again believer." Never in my life had I ever felt so peaceful and yet so filled with joy. I wanted to talk about it. I wanted to tell somebody—anybody. I tried to call my family, and no one answered the phone. Tyrone's mother, whom I called Mom, had become a Christian recently, so I phoned her. I *had* to talk to another Christian, and to share this wonderful joy.

"Listen, Mom, guess what? I got saved. I'm a Christian now!"

"Praise the Lord!" she thundered back. "Oh, Ullanda, I've been praying for you ever since I first got saved."

A week later, I was back in my New York apartment. It was late, but Tyrone had waited up, delighted to have me back. I was a little uneasy because I hadn't told Tyrone that I'd given my life to Jesus. Finally it was time to go to bed, and I still hadn't said anything to him about being a Christian. When he pulled me close and started to kiss me, I pushed him away.

"What's wrong?" he asked.

"I can't do this any more," I said. "I can't live this way."

"What do you mean?" He reached out to stroke my cheek, but I pulled back even farther.

"I'm now a born-again Christian."

"What are you talking about?" He didn't understand. He'd never gone to church. No matter how hard I tried to make him understand, he had nothing in his life to relate to my experience. I started to get frustrated. "I can't explain it to you. Call your mother. She understands, because she's a Christian now. She'll be able to explain it to you."

"OK," he said, "I'll do that tomorrow. In the meantime, tell me your plans now that you've changed. What's going to happen to us? To you?"

"I'm going to move out."

"What do you mean by that? Why would you want to move out?"

"Haven't you heard a word I said?"

"Sure, I heard you. I don't understand, but I'm trying to."

We began to argue. Finally he stopped me, and said, "Wait, Ullanda, let's talk about this."

"There's nothing more to talk about," I said. "I'm a Christian. I can't live this lifestyle any longer." By then I was so angry, I ran upstairs.

Hurriedly I started throwing things into suitcases. Tyrone came, saw what I was doing, and we continued to argue. I yelled at him for the first time in our four years together. At that he grabbed me and slapped me several times—something he'd never done before.

"Jesus! Help me!" I had never uttered those words before, but they came from the depth of my heart.

A startled look crossed his face as he realized what he'd done. He released me, turned around, and went downstairs. I followed him. He fell on the living room floor and began to sob.

"It's all right," I said, touched at his sudden tenderness. "It's going to be all right."

"I'm sorry I hit you," Tyrone said through his tears. "I don't know what got into me. I swear it will never happen again. You started talking so strange, and then you started to pack your things—you scared me. I don't want to lose you."

By then, I had melted too.

Our voices grew quiet and calm. I tried to explain, to help him understand the importance of Jesus Christ in my life.

"Ullanda, don't leave," he said at last. "Right now, I can't understand what's happened to you. But I'll do whatever you want and whatever it takes if you won't leave me." He held me tightly.

"It's all right," I said. "Somehow we'll work this out."

I promised to stay.

Side by side on the living room floor, we fell asleep.

• • •

One thing I appreciated about Ashford and Simpson was that before every concert, they gathered all of us inside their dressing room and we prayed. They'd been doing this for about 10 years. I deeply respected both of them. They tried to keep Christ in their lives and in the program by insisting that all of us join them in prayer.

They'd been brought up in the church, although I didn't know much about their background. One time Nick Ashford said he had been a bum on the street begging for quarters and sleeping in the parks or other public places in New York City. When he reached the end of his resources he said that he prayed for God's help. Afterward he felt impressed to go to church, and he did. From that day on, his life began to change. He met Valerie Simpson at that church. They began writing songs together and later they married.

Before my conversion, the praying before concerts hadn't meant much to me, although I thought it was a nice thing to do. After my conversion, I began to think, *Oh, what a beautiful and wonderful thing we do together.*

I continued to tour with Ashford and Simpson for another three months. I wanted to talk to everyone about my new-found relationship with Jesus Christ. But how? What should I say? I couldn't even explain to myself what had happened, so I decided not to say anything to others until I had it figured out.

Grandfather Jones had brought me up to know how

Christians were expected to live. He had ingrained in me that Christians just did not do certain things—things that were part of the lifestyle I'd been living for many years. So what should I do now? I asked God again and again to guide me. I decided that after this tour, I wouldn't go on the road with them again because of the kind of music we did—mostly rhythm and blues. But it was more than the music. I remembered Tramaine, who'd said she couldn't be involved with The Honeycomb because of the sensual dancing and sexy clothes. Grandfather Jones was dead, but he would have said, "Ullanda, a Christian should not behave in such a manner." On her last visit to New York, Sonja had spoken strongly about how Christians were to live.

Yet the lifestyle I had to turn away from was the lifestyle of most of my friends. Adultery was so commonplace, no one took it seriously as being something wrong. The people I mingled with seemed to be in and out of sexual affairs every third week. In the music business, no one had trouble finding drugs—they were everywhere. Musicians and singers can't have a bad day when they perform, so many of them used drugs as their way to be "up" for every performance. I knew that I had to leave that world because I no longer belonged to it. But then what? Without anyone saying a word, I knew that to follow Christ, I had to change my lifestyle.

I had to change. And if I changed, then what would happen? The answers to those questions scared me.

● ● ●

Although I didn't talk about Jesus to the people I toured with, inside I knew I had changed. I felt at peace with myself. I found it easier to treat people nicer and I felt more open to them. Most of all, I knew I was converted and Christ was dwelling within me.

Before long, band members saw a difference in me and one of them commented, "Hey, you've become nicer to us these last few days. What's happened?

"I'm seeing life a little differently now," I said.

"Keep it up!"

"Count on it!" I said.

• • •

God has a plan for me. Just to think it encouraged me immensely. Each day I grew more aware of how God was leading me. One significant thing on the trip involved Ann, the Caucasian girlfriend of one of the Black band members. She was a lovely model, and basically a nice person. Previously I'd looked down on the band members' groupie girl friends, for their behavior disgusted me. Even after I began to change, I still had no interest in getting to know any of those girls.

But this particular girl seemed different. Or maybe I became interested in her because I was different now. I felt strongly that I needed to talk to her and that she needed help. Soon she and I became friends, and I saw her often during the time we stayed in Southern California. Before long she began to open up to me. Often she would break down and cry, and I was able to talk to her about the comfort that only God can bring and the inner wounds that only God can heal. The morning we left to start East, I found a note she had slipped under my hotel door. She had written, *Ullanda, you are such a blessing to me. I really want to thank you for being so kind.*

I thought, *this being nice to people means so much to them.* Before I had been nasty and intolerant, looking down my nose at those no-good little groupies. Now I understood. God loved them! They were no different from Ullanda McCullough, because God loves everyone. I began to cry.

Chapter 20

. . . .

Ullanda, I was convinced you would never make it," Sonja said when I told her about my conversion. "I thought you were going to be lost forever."

"God honored your prayers anyway," I said.

"When I left your apartment to go home," she said, and smiled in embarrassment, "I felt really discouraged. I had tried so hard to talk to you about the Lord. On the plane, I felt so downhearted that I told the Lord, 'Lord, forget it, she's not a candidate. She's after the world, and she's never going to change.' I'm glad I was wrong."

My good news elated the Christians in my family. They surrounded me, trying to encourage me. They offered suggestions to help me grow and avoid the failures and pitfalls of others. In their zeal, they confused me by telling me things I should do and what I needed to avoid. I had become free by turning to Jesus Christ, and now it seemed as if everyone wanted to chain me by telling me all the things I could and couldn't do.

After listening to all the advice, I said, "I've heard everything you've told me, and I'm still new at all this, so I'm going to have to pray for the Lord to show me exactly what to do."

"That's the way to do it," said Aunt Gladys who'd been a Christian all her life. "Then you'll know for certain what God wants."

. . .

What do I do now? I had to change my lifestyle, and I was already making changes as I understood what God wanted from me.

But I hadn't yet faced my big issues. First, my work. Did God want me to leave everything I'd worked to build up for the past 10 years? I didn't want to offend people or start preaching to them, but I didn't want to keep silent about my faith in Jesus Christ. Could I stay in the business and still be a committed Christian?

What about Tyrone? Stay together? Break up? Insist we get married? No answer seemed right, so I knew it meant I had to pray until God showed me what to do. For a while I didn't have anyone in New York to talk to. Even after my conversion, I was still living with Tyrone, trying to figure out how to get out of the relationship.

Tyrone was open to my new life, and I didn't want to demand more than he was ready to handle. He agreed to attend an Apostolic Church (Pentecostal), went with me and seemed to enjoy the services. Soon we were attending every Sunday and going back Wednesday night for prayer meeting.

Tyrone finally had an idea of what it meant that I was a Christian, changing in a number of ways. Even when he didn't fully understand, he remained supportive. More than once he said, "Fine, fine, no problem. I can accept that."

As I surveyed my life, I said aloud, "This really *is* the good life. Everything is going just right for me. Tyrone is following Jesus too."

I still knew little about the Christian faith, but I was learning. The first thing to confront me was that Tyrone and I were still living together. But I didn't know how I could move out without hurting Tyrone. For many people, it might have been an easy thing to say, "This is sin, and I'm through." Maybe that would have been the best thing to do, but I did what I felt was the most caring thing for Tyrone. He'd begun to turn to God and remained supportive of my growth. I'd been exposed to the faith as a child, I reasoned, and knew how I was to live. But this was a new way of life to him. Slowly he was coming around, a step at a time. I felt confident God would show him at the right time.

One day a woman at the church spoke to Tyrone about his conversion, and she encouraged him to grow. As they talked, she told him that she had been observing him for weeks, and it concerned her that he didn't seem to be moving along the spiritual pathway very rapidly. At some point during their talk, she asked him about me, "Is Ullanda your wife?"

"Oh, no, we're not married."

"Is she your girlfriend?"

"Yes, that's right."

"But you live together, don't you?"

"Oh, yeah, sure we do."

"Well, that's your problem, Tyrone. Don't you know you're not supposed to be living with a woman who is not your wife?"

"Oh, really?" he asked. "You're sure?"

"Definitely. The Bible says it's wrong."

"I didn't know that. Or at least I didn't understand that part. You see, until Ullanda brought me here, I had never been to church in my life."

Later that afternoon, when Tyrone and I were together, he told me what the woman had said. "Is it true that we're not supposed to be living together? Was she right?"

"Tyrone, the woman was correct about our living together." I was so excited that he asked. Finally God had spoken.

"So what do we do?" he asked.

"What do you think the Lord wants us to do?"

"Let's pray," he said. "God will show us."

I got off the bed where we were seated, and knelt in prayer. I asked God to guide us.

When I finished, Tyrone said, "If we live together, we're supposed to be married. Right? That means that either we need to get married or we separate."

"That's our choice," I said.

Tyrone still wasn't ready to get married, so he knew what he had to do. "I'll move out tomorrow."

He had kept his own apartment, so we had no big hassle to go through.

Although we'd no longer live together, we agreed to continue to date and attend church together. True to his word, Tyrone had all his things laid out when I got back from a session the next day.

Everything seemed to be working fine. We decided to attend a nondenominational church called the Unbroken Chain where a number of actors, models, and singers from New York worshiped. We felt more at home with our own kind of people.

One time when we walked into the Unbroken Chain, a beautiful model saw us. She ran up to us and screamed, "I can't believe it! Am I seeing things? Tyrone Spears is a Christian?"

"I sure am," he said and hugged her.

• • •

I needed to be part of the Unbroken Chain in those days. I felt accepted and I needed the warmth of a caring congregation. They knew the kind of problems people in our business faced, and we could talk openly about them. Just to know we could unload and people would understand was a big help to me.

Among the special individuals I met was Gay Thomas, a former girlfriend of Tyrone's. Soon Gay and I became friends. Often the three of us would talk about the Lord. She encouraged Tyrone not to let up on his spiritual growth. Several times she said, "You and Ullanda need to get together and get married. With the Lord's help, you can work things out."

• • •

"What's next for me?" I asked God every single day. I knew that God would show me when to leave the jingle business, and how. And what about Tyrone and me? Did God want us to get married? It seemed the natural thing to do, and yet I wasn't sure.

In the meantime, while I waited for God's guidance, I developed several Christian friendships. My closest friend had been Yvonne Lewis, another jingle singer. One day during a session, when I told her that I'd become a Christian, she reminded me that she was a Christian, too, a member of the Seventh-day Adventist Church. She had fallen away from the church shortly after we met and hadn't been involved in it for 10 years. But she said, "Lala (her nickname for me), I still feel close to God. And so I recently returned to church."

Over the ensuing weeks, Yvonne and I had many conversations about God. The more we talked together, the closer we became. Then an old friend from Detroit, Dennis Collins, started to hang out with us. Back in Detroit, our families knew each other well.

The three of us starting meeting at Yvonne's Manhattan apartment just to talk about God. Nothing planned, but it just happened. And I loved going there. For hours sometimes, we talked and shared what God was doing. Each of us also sought guidance for our lives.

"We need to be sharing our faith with others," Dennis said on one of those occasions so we decided to have a Bible study-prayer meeting every Friday in Yvonne's apartment.

When we started our Friday night fellowship, in the fall of 1985, we welcomed anybody who believed in Jesus Christ or was open to learn more about Him. We sang a lot of songs and had testimonies. Someone described it as an informal church service.

Meetings began about 7:00 p.m. and we tried to finish by 10:00, although a few stayed as late as midnight. At first, we invited only our closest friends, and most of them came. Then we extended our invitation to others in the business, some we hardly knew. A few of them came. Some were big names and others virtually unknown, but in that apartment, all differences vanished.

Roberta Flack came several Friday evenings and was quite open about herself. If I remember correctly, she said her grandmother reared her in church, but like many of us, she had slipped away. Stephanie Mills was another big name in the business, and she came whenever she could.

Usually we would sit and talk informally for a while on issues and problems. At times we invited pastors to speak. Sometimes we scheduled seminars on various topics. Most of the time, however, we chose a book in the Bible to study. To begin, we chose the Gospel of John, going through a chapter a week. If we had, say 30 people, each person would read a verse until we finished the chapter. Then we discussed how we could apply what we'd read to our lives. Sometimes the verses would spark someone to say, "This reminds me of something I've gone through this week. And this is how the Bible helped me cope."

About the same time that we started Friday night meetings, Yvonne's grandmother urged her to go back to the Ephesus Seventh-day Adventist Church. They had a new pastor named

Clement Murray. She said, "You'll like this man so much." Yvonne decided to go once to please her grandmother.

Grandmother was right—she did like him. Largely because of the pastor, Yvonne renewed her commitment to God, became active, and never left the church again.

At Yvonne's invitation, I also began to attend the Ephesus Seventh-day Adventist Church, a spacious brick structure with three steeples and a large, black, wrought-iron gate. Located at the corner of 123rd Street at Lenox in Harlem, the church had beautiful stained glass windows. The building seats about 2,000 people, with a large balcony and upstairs choir loft. The mammoth pipe organ impressed me immensely.

Like Yvonne, I enjoyed the Ephesus Church. However, this brought about new problems. On Saturday I attended Ephesus Church with Yvonne; on Sunday I went to Unbroken Chain. Both churches insisted they worshiped on the *right* day. Frankly, it didn't matter to me, but I wanted to follow God's leading. *What is the right day for me to worship?* In the Old Testament, I read several places, especially in the Ten Commandments, that the people of God were to worship on the Sabbath, the seventh day of the week. Adventists taught that since this command was not revoked in the New Testament, it's as valid as any other of the Ten Commandments, and I never found any verse that said I should worship on Sunday.

I also realized that I was a Christian and justified by the merits of Christ, no matter what day I went to church. Often I prayed, "God, I'm going to get this thing right about the day to worship. Whatever you want me to do, I'll do it." Because I was confused, I decided, *Well, for now, I'll just go both days.* So I went with Yvonne on Saturday to Ephesus and on Sunday I went with Dennis and Tyrone to the Unbroken Chain.

• • •

More and more my life revolved around church activities. And with Bible study, choir rehearsals, and prayer meetings, I had some kind of church involvement every night of the week except Thursday. I loved being busy. However, my frantic schedule eventually began to bend me out of shape. As I reviewed my situation, I realized I was learning toward the Adventists, although I liked both churches. Both pastors preached strong, biblical messages. But at Ephesus I felt more accepted, although I couldn't explain why. Another thing that attracted me about Adventists is that they presented to their members the challenge of living a healthful lifestyle. They stressed health and fitness and the importance of taking care of our bodies, the temple of the Holy Spirit. Many of them were vegetarians. Because I had been a vegetarian since 1974, this was one more link that bonded me to the Adventists, and made me feel even more at home among them. As I compared what they taught and what I heard in other churches I visited, I felt the SDA church was teaching their members to live by all of God's commands, especially salvation by grace through Jesus in Jesus Christ. And for me, I soon also began to believe that God's commands included honoring the Sabbath.

Since Tyrone and I were finally going to get married, it seemed right that the choice of church should be his as much as mine. I asked him, "Are you interested in joining the Adventist Church?"

"Not really," he admitted.

I didn't push. But it did confuse me. I was growing more convinced that I belonged at the Ephesus Church and Tyrone liked going to the Unbroken Chain.

So what should I do? I couldn't take the next step of joining a church until God guided me. "I know you'll show me, God. And I'm willing to wait until you do."

Chapter 21

. . . .

I could do that, I told myself. At the Ephesus Church they called it Project Ingathering and the more I thought about it, the more I thought, *why not?*

A friend explained that once a year she and others went out on the streets and talked to people about Jesus Christ and the mission of the church in other parts of the world. They also handed out pamphlets. It impressed me when I learned that they collected donations for emergency help overseas as well as disaster relief in North America. They joined with the more than four million Adventists all over the world, who gave to this fund to alleviate human suffering.

I wanted to join them, to share my faith, and invite others to give money to help the needy. But my new friend hesitated.

"Well, you see, Ullanda, we do want volunteers, but we have certain dress codes that we go by." It was obvious she didn't want to hurt my feelings. "If you're out there representing the Seventh-day Adventist Church, there's a certain way to conduct yourself." She seemed flustered, but added, "You know, your jewelry and all."

"What do you mean?" I asked, confused. "I'm always dressed up and I try to look nice."

"That's not what I mean," she said. "You see, we believe in modest dress. You're wearing beautiful things—but, well, they're very extravagant. Your jewels, especially that gorgeous diamond bracelet and earrings. There's nothing wrong with them except we feel we can be better witnesses by being modestly attired."

"Really?" I asked in surprise. "I've never heard of anything like that before." I stared at her. For the first time it registered that she didn't wear makeup. Those who wore makeup, wore it lightly. A watch was the only jewelry she wore.

"I hope you understand, but we believe in being temperate in all things. For us that includes being moderately dressed."

"Can you show me in the Bible where it says you're not supposed to wear makeup and jewelry? I've just never heard this before, that's all."

"I don't know the texts right off hand, but I can find out, and I'll get back to you." Tyrone came up to us then, and we left the church and got into the car. He was driving, so it gave me an opportunity to search through my Bible. *God, if this is in the Bible, show me.* Just as I breathed that prayer, my Bible fell open at the Ten Commandments in Exodus 20. I read them through, thinking maybe there was something there. But I didn't read anything about jewelry or makeup. *What was she talking about?*

As Tyrone drove, I kept going back to the first commandment, "Thou shalt have no other gods before me"* *That doesn't say anything.* Rapidly I scanned my Bible, moving from Proverbs and Psalms to the letters of Paul in the New Testament. I couldn't find anything on jewelry. *She doesn't know what she's talking about.* In disgust I closed the Bible and prayed, "Lord, if it's in here, please show me where I have to let go of my jewelry." I told God I was going to open the Bible and try once again. *If it's there, then you show me.* When I opened the Bible, again it fell open to Exodus 20. Again I read, "Thou shalt have no other gods before me."

I don't have any other gods before You or beside You. Now I really felt confused. *God, are you trying to show me something? Trying to speak to me? What do you mean by thou shalt have no other gods before me?* Then a thought hit me: *My jewelry.* I had been worshiping diamonds and baubles. All my expensive clothing became the way to display the jewelry.

Oh, no, I wanted to scream, that can't be true. Not that.

---

* Exodus 20:3

Certainly not. Yet I knew it was true. Every month I spent thousands of dollars just on jewelry. One bracelet, for instance, a small gold one with diamonds, cost me $5,000, and that was the wholesale price. Instinctively, I glanced at the bracelet. I had owned it seven years and never went out of the apartment without it. Frequently I wore expensive furs and exclusive designer clothes.

Yes, Lord, that's right. I do worship this bracelet, don't I? In just one instant, I realized what God was trying to tell me. Jewels, clothes, and things like that had become my god. I lived for them—or I had until Jesus Christ came into my life. Now it was time to put them away if I wanted to serve God.

Lord, if that's what you're telling me I have to do for me to be a Christian both inwardly and outwardly, okay. I don't need all this stuff to make me feel good about myself anymore. As proof to God of my serious intentions, I wanted to take off the bracelet and drop it inside my purse and never wear it again. But I needed another sign to be certain. Then, I knew, I would feel at peace.

• • •

Give it to Valerie! The command just popped into my head. It came from that deep, interior voice I had now begun to recognize.

"What?" I asked. I could hardly believe that was God speaking to me, and yet I knew it was. The impression came exactly a week after I felt God wanted me to stop wearing jewelry. I'd just bought a beautiful study Bible for Dennis as he'd commented that he wanted to have one. I said to myself right then, *Fine, I'll buy it for him as a surprise gift.* At the moment, I heard those words, "Give it to Valerie," I was driving to Dennis's apartment to give him the Bible.

Not to Dennis. Give it to Valerie. Stop at Valerie's house and take her the Bible.

"No, this can't be right," I said. "This can't be God speaking. I bought this Bible for Dennis."

Along with the Bible, give her your bracelet.

"I'm not getting rid of my bracelet. I can't let go of this bracelet. This one piece of jewelry means too much to me. *I won't wear it anymore, God, I promise. But I've had it so long, and I do love it.* Besides, why should I give it to Valerie?"

No matter how much I struggled internally, I knew that was what I had to do. My own words condemned me, because I had blurted out loud, "I do love it." Yet it didn't make sense. Valerie didn't need more jewelry, and she probably didn't need a Bible either. Despite my arguments, I had no peace.

"OK, God, I'll do this because I think that's what you want me to do."

I parked in front of Valerie's brownstone. After I rang the bell, her maid came to the door. She told me Valerie was out and wouldn't be back until late. As I listened, I felt myself shaking inside, wondering what I was doing there anyway. It didn't make sense, and yet I knew what I had to do. I handed her the nicely-wrapped Bible and said, "Would you please give this to Valerie for me?" She looked at me strangely and before she could say anything, I said, "Oh, and will you give this to her as well?" I handed her my gorgeous bracelet. I stared at it for only a second. It had been such a part of me, and now I was getting rid of it— one more bondage broken in my life.

"Yes, surely," she said, but the strange look didn't leave her face.

"And please ask Valerie to call me, will you?" I walked back to my car. I was shaking nervously and felt I would burst into tears if I didn't get myself under control. I couldn't understand why God would want me to give away my beautiful bracelet. I had promised not to wear it anymore. Wasn't that enough?

This made no sense whatsoever and I prayed for strength and understanding. Then I remembered a verse, "In all your ways acknowledge him, and he will make your paths straight."*

I had obeyed God. That's what mattered.

Peace slowly came over me.

Two days later Valerie called, puzzled. "Ullanda, what's going on?" she asked.

Only weeks before I'd visited her and told her that I had been born again and couldn't go on the road with them anymore. She was happy for me and understood. At that time she'd said something sweet that really touched me. "We're happy for

---

* Proverbs 3:6, NIV

you. But I want you to know that as far as we're concerned, you were always a Christian. Why, after the concerts you'd go straight to your room. You didn't smoke or drink or run around. You didn't socialize, so we thought you were a Christian."

Now she repeated her question, "What's going on with the Bible and bracelet?"

"I don't really know what I meant by giving you the Bible and bracelet," I said, "but I do know this. I was leaving church Saturday and I was impressed to give the bracelet and Bible to you."

"But, Ullanda, that's your favorite bracelet. You spent a lot of money for it, and I know how much it means to you."

"But you see, Valerie, it's no longer important. The Lord impressed me to give it to you. If you're bothered, you pray and ask God why."

"I think you need to take it back."

"I can't. God told me to give it to you."

"All right," Valerie said, "but it sure sounds strange to me."

A month later she called again. "Ullanda, I want to meet you for lunch. I've got to see you. It's about the bracelet. I'll explain it then."

When we met the following week she held out the bracelet. "Here. Take it back."

"I can't do that."

"Listen, it's causing me a lot of grief. Take it."

"What are you talking about?"

"This bracelet haunts me. Every time I look at it, I think of you and of your conversion and what you're doing now. You know, giving up your career for the Lord. Then you turn around and give me this and the Bible."

"Something's working then," I said and smiled. I thought maybe that's why God wanted me to give it to her.

Valerie told me that she'd started attending a nearby church and felt at home there. None of them knew she was a famous singer and songwriter. As the years have passed, both Nick and Valerie have been highly successful. And they still have a love for God and attend church as often as possible.

Valerie wasn't through with me, though. "I want this bracelet out of my house," she said, putting it in my hand. Then said that the more she tried not to think about the bracelet, the more it intruded into her life. It reminded her of me and the changes I'd made in my life. And that made her feel uncomfortable.

When she finished her story, Valerie stared at me. "Ullanda, what is going on?"

I laughed. "Maybe God is trying to speak to you."

"Maybe, but I just don't want this around. I want it out of my house and out of my life."

I still protested. "Valerie, don't give that bracelet to me. The Lord didn't tell me to take this bracelet back."

"Please take it. I don't want it."

"I can't take it. I had to get it out of my life."

"And now I want it out of mine!"

"Do this. Hold on to the bracelet," I said. "I'll pray about it. If the Lord tells me to take it, then you can give it to me. OK?"

"This is ridiculous, Ullanda, and you're really taking me through a lot."

I stood my ground and a few days later, Valerie phoned again. "You have to take this bracelet. I won't keep it. It's expensive, it's not mine, and you have to take it back."

When I protested, she said, "Ullanda, whatever the Lord has to do with me I guess He's done it now, so please take this bracelet."

Perhaps she was right. By giving her my prized piece of jewelry, I had broken its power over me. Now things such as jewelry meant nothing to me. I had won victory over my false gods.

So I took the bracelet back from Valerie.

Chapter 22

● ● ● ● ● ● ● ● ● ● ● ● ● ● ● ● ● ● ●

I was still doing jingles, but I didn't feel totally good about it any more.

"God," I often prayed, "it's so hard for me to live for You while I'm still here in New York with all these temptations around me. Please, get me away from here. Send me to some place where I can study and get rooted in the faith. I know You have something better for me to do. Please show me."

The beginning of the answer came for me through two new friends, Judy and Todd Glascow. They told me about a kind of health institute in Seale, Alabama, called Uchee Pines. Todd explained that people go there to learn how to live more healthful lives.

"This may be the place you've been looking for," Judy said. "If you could afford to spend a little time there, you'd be able to get the teaching and grounding you want." Two SDA doctors operated Uchee Pines as a nonprofit organization, and the place had won the respect and approval of the Adventist Church. They also offered excellent Bible classes and a range of other subjects, such as hydrotherapy and how to grow your own food. It sounded like the perfect place for me, and it would get me out of New York for a while.

But was it right to go? Tyrone and I were still engaged, but the relationship wasn't going well. We continued to talk about marriage, but I had a nagging, inner feeling that we were moving toward a breakup.

"I want to get married at the Ephesus Church," I finally

said. "Is that OK?"

That didn't bother him, although he preferred the Unbroken Chain.

But when I said that we'd need to go for pre-marital counseling with Pastor Murray, he dug in his heels. He saw no need for it and, in fact, I think was afraid of it.

We discussed this at some length. He insisted that he loved me and didn't want to lose me, but he didn't see a need for counseling before we married.

Yvonne talked to me about our marriage plans. "Lala, I know that you love him," she said. "But if you marry him, and it's not the Lord's will, you'll both be miserable. I'm telling you this from my own experience. The first time, I married the wrong man and for years my life was a mess. Then I married a second time and now I find myself going through another difficult divorce. I didn't ask God to guide my life. Know why I married him? Because he was handsome and funny, made me laugh, and we had a lot of fun times together. Now the fun is over. I'm back in the church, and the church isn't for him." She paused and wiped away her tears, and then said, "Oh, Lala, I want the best for you. Please don't make the mistakes I did. Don't let it happen to you."

Yvonne had suffered so much through her two failed marriages. It touched me deeply that she didn't want me to make a mistake.

I phoned my sister Verbena, now a Christian, too, and told her my concern. "I'm going to put you in my prayers and ask my church to pray for you," she said. "And, Ullanda, I'm going to do something else. I'm going to fast for you for three days. By the end of the three days, I'm asking the Lord to impress you so strongly you'll know what to do."

During the time she was fasting, Tyrone and I were discussing our marriage plans. I studied the Bible every free minute I had. Never before had I prayed so much or so intensely.

The more Tyrone and I talked, the wider the gap grew between us. I felt that being a Christian meant separating myself from the world. Tyrone insisted that he could be a committed Christian and still enjoy the worldly lifestyle, such as the parties we used to attend.

His attitude hurt me. Maybe I was more zealous, I don't

know, but I realized that we were headed in different directions. If something drastic didn't happen, I knew we would continue to move away from each other.

"Ullanda, I don't have any problem with your going to church as often as you want. Go every night if that's what you want. Do whatever you want to do for the Lord. That's fine, and I'll support you. But you have to understand that I won't go to every event at the church or get as involved as you are. Sometimes I'll choose not to go to things."

"It's not going to work," I told him sadly. "I need a husband who will be as zealous and involved as I am. That means that if we married, it would be disastrous for both of us."

He became angry and charged me with wanting to drop him from my life. "How can you do this to me? I moved out of your apartment. I've gone along with everything you've asked. I go to church. I've turned to God, but I can't give any more."

"I'm sorry, but —"

"This isn't the way Jesus Christ wants you to treat me. You just can't do this."

"Talk to your mother, Tyrone. Maybe she can explain why I have to do what I'm doing. When she explains, you'll be able to understand."

His mother tried to explain that I was doing what the Lord wanted me to do. "She's convicted by God in ways you're not. And, son, unless you're willing to make the same kind of commitment, it won't work for either of you."

They talked on the phone a long time. Finally, Tyrone accepted it, but he wasn't happy.

"It's not going to work," I said between my tears. "I can't go your way. For me to do that would make me a kind of half-Christian. There are things that don't bother you, but they don't fit the lifestyle God is calling me to live."

We didn't actually break up, but I think both of us realized that it had been settled.

Afterward, I called Verbena and told her what had been said and thanked her for fasting for me. The Lord had answered her prayers.

That same evening we were going out with Herschel Walker,

the famous football player, and his wife, Cindy. Herschel was the guest of honor at a banquet and Tyrone begged me to dress up, to look good for him in front of his friends. He pled with me to wear an evening gown and my jewelry, and to fix my makeup like I'd done in the past.

I could tell this was important, but I held back. "I just don't think God wants me to dress that way."

"Please," he pleaded. "Just this one time, and I won't ask you to do it again. This is such a big affair and I don't want to be embarrassed."

"Embarrassed?" That made me angry and hurt, but I tried to see the situation from his perspective. After we talked some more, I said, "OK, I'm upset and I really don't want to do this. But we promised weeks ago to be there. So I'll get dressed the way I used to—just for you—just for tonight."

So I got dressed up for Tyrone. I wore my diamond earrings, the bracelet Valerie had given back to me, and my most expensive evening gown. I suppose I looked beautiful. But I felt miserable.

Tyrone spent the evening showing me off. He just wouldn't get off the topic of clothes and makeup. I knew he was trying to tell me that this was the way I should always look so he could be proud of me and want to show me off.

But when he took me home, I said, "Tyrone, I'm angry. How could you embarrass me that way?"

"I just want you to look your best. When we go out with our friends, we have to look the part. We can't look sick or shabby."

"That's the problem. You want fame and fortune. You want to hang out with all these famous people, but I can't live this kind of life anymore. I've been there and I don't need these things. I just don't see that we have any future together because I can't go your way, and you can't go mine. Don't you see we'd be miserable?"

For weeks I had asked God for the answer. Now I had it, but it wasn't the one I had wanted.

• • •

My life took another sharp turn through the ministry of Wintley Phipps. An outstanding singer and pastor of Capitol Hill

Seventh-day Adventist Church in Washington, D.C., he came to Brooklyn to do a concert. Yvonne and I went because Arthur Andrews, a lay minister friend, invited us. We were so impressed with Wintley that we spoke to him after the concert. During the conversation, we mentioned that we were professional singers in the jingle business and he asked us to sing for him when he did his next project.

A short time later, he called Yvonne and invited us to come up for a Saturday in November. As I sat in the congregation that Sabbath, I wore a modest, but colorful, Koos dress with matching coat and hat. By now I felt comfortable without jewelry or make-up. As strange as it may sound, dressing differently made me feel I was truly becoming the kind of person God wanted me to be.

Pastor Phipps preached a powerful sermon about baptism and announced they would have a baptismal service afterward. His words challenged and energized me. As I listened intently, I heard that quiet inner voice saying, "This is the Church where you belong. This is where you need to be baptized." Immediately a powerful urge to be baptized came over me. I felt that God had cleansed me in a way I had not understood before when I let go of my jewelry. So what should I do? I had learned much more about God's word and His will for my life. So many things had now become clear. I was ready to go forward, and I believed I needed to do this again.

This can't be the voice of the Lord, I thought. *I was baptized some time back, after I gave my heart to Jesus Christ. If I go up now for another baptism they're all going to think I'm crazy.* Yet in my heart I heard God's voice, and I couldn't ignore it. I really believe it was God speaking to me. As I sat there I tried to reason out why I shouldn't be baptized again. Adventists require six weeks of biblical teaching before baptism. I'd been baptized into Christ before, but had not been instructed, and felt I had moved ahead of God's leading. If I received baptism today, it meant I was committing myself to join the Adventist Church. *Is this what I want to do? Is this what God is leading me to do?*

Pastor Phipps instructed us to close our eyes, bow our heads, and pray for those among us who needed to turn to Jesus Christ. At the very moment my struggle became the most intense, he said, "If there is anyone else in the congregation today who wants to be baptized, raise your hand ." I hesitated, knowing Yvonne would think it strange. Then Pastor Phipps, as if reading my mind, said, "If you feel impressed by the Holy Spirit to be baptized, don't sit there and fight it. Raise your hand and give your life to the Lord. He'll work everything out for you." Shortly after that, those who raised their hands were asked to go to the front and fill out a card.

I went to the front and the church clerk took my name and address. She suggested I might prefer to return to New York and be baptized in my church after I had completed the six weeks of instruction.

"No, no, please," I said. "I want to be baptized today."

"Today?" She stared at me. Apparently she had not encountered this kind of situation before.

"I feel impressed to be baptized today. I've had some serious changes in my life, and I want to be baptized as a symbol of my total surrender. This is something I have to do."

"OK, one second." She left. After a couple of minutes she came back and took my name. "All right," she said, "I've arranged it."

I went upstairs where the candidates were waiting and they fitted me with a white robe and white cap. All nine of us walked into the sanctuary and sat down on the front row. My friends were sitting immediately behind me.

Yvonne tapped me on my shoulder and whispered, "What are you doing?"

I didn't answer.

"Are you getting baptized?"

I still didn't speak.

"You can't do that," she whispered. "You've been baptized. Besides, you're not going to join this church."

You may not understand or even agree, I said to myself, *but I have to do this. I'm doing this out of obedience to God.* But I didn't answer Yvonne aloud, only patted her hand and smiled.

A few minutes later she leaned forward again and whispered, "Ullanda, are you trying to mock the church? Are you trying to make fun of the church?" Her voice had become agitated, and I understood her point of view, but I still said nothing. Again I patted her hand. She finally leaned back and didn't try to stop me again.

As I sat there, I knew I was going contrary to what others believed. Yet I felt it was something I had to do for myself.

The eight candidates stepped into the pool, one at a time and received baptism. Just as I came forward, Pastor Phipps stared at me, clearly surprised. The secretary had told him who I was, but the name must not have registered, and now he didn't seem to know what to do. From our conversation, he knew I had not gone through the Bible classes. He and the elder who assisted him stared at each other, and the seconds ticked away.

Having been brought up in a Pentecostal church, and knowing that people went into the baptismal pool full of enthusiasm and praise, I did just what I had seen done in Grandfather Jones's church and at the Greater Refuge Temple. I started praising the Lord, shouting such things as, "Oh, thank you Jesus! Glory, hallelujah!" They came from my heart!

Pastor Phipps must have thought I had lost control of myself. He grabbed my hand and tried to explain to me that he was going to cover my mouth. "Just relax," he whispered.

All the while I was still screaming, "Thank you, Jesus!"

He stopped trying to instruct me. He had to do something to regain control of the situation and quiet me. Apparently he decided to go ahead and baptize me and get me out of this pool, because I was creating a scene. He put his hand over my mouth and dipped me into the water. When I came up, I was still shouting, "Hallejuah! Praise the Lord! Thank you, Jesus!"

They got me out of the pool and away from the congregation as quickly as possible. Naturally Yvonne felt embarrassed. The members of the congregation didn't know how to respond to my emotional display. I can't blame them, because this was certainly not the way they conducted baptismal services.

But at the time, I was unaware of their reaction. My heart was filled with joy because I had obeyed God. I kept hearing the words of Jesus inside my heart, "If you love me, keep my commandments." *

---

* John 14:15—obey God rather than man.

After I changed out of the robe, I came downstairs. Yvonne was waiting for me. She shook her head, "Ullanda, I can't believe what I saw. Do you really know what you've done?"

"I was following the Lord," I said, "even if you don't understand. This is what I felt impressed to do." I tried to explain that in my zeal to follow Jesus Christ, my previous baptism had come about because I rushed ahead of God's leading. "As far as I'm concerned, this counts as my one and only baptism." I was not aware that many churches accept baptism only once.*

I knew little theology then, yet I knew some would want to argue with me and try to convince me how wrong I was. But I had responded to the Spirit of God dealing with me. Now I had done it. I had read that it is better to obey God rather than man.

Yvonne remained unsure for a while because she believed I shouldn't have undergone baptism.

Poor Pastor Phipps. "This isn't normally the procedure here," he said to me afterward, "but it has been done. So I'll be praying for you to remain faithful to God."

One of the elders asked the pastor, "How is she supposed to take classes? She lives in New York."

The church clerk said she would contact the Ephesus Church, and I could be instructed there. "I know you were sincere, Ullanda," she said. "And I think that's what counts the most. You did this because you are trying to serve the Lord."

"Thank you," I said. She had understood.

But most of all, I believed God had understood.

---

* Some churches I visited did allow baptism for those who turned from the gospel, left the church, and then came back and recommitted their lives to God.

Chapter 23

Leaving New York, Tyrone, and the music business was easier than I had expected. I didn't cry or even feel sad. In fact, I felt so excited about a change of direction in my life, I could hardly wait to get away.

For the next few days I kept my mind on Uchee Pines and refused to dwell on the breakup. Lovely Christian friends, Judy and Todd Glasco, were encouraging me to go and I gladly took their advice. I'd sold my expensive clothing and jewelry. I also took care of my business transactions, part of which included breaking my partnership with TySpears Cosmetics. I loaned my furniture to Dennis Collins because he had not yet bought any for his lovely apartment on upper Fifth Avenue.

He and Yvonne promised to keep the Friday night meetings going. They also insisted on giving me a going-away party before I left for Uchee Pines. About 50 people came, including pastor Clement Murray of Ephesus Church. During that special evening, we prayed and sang and rejoiced. Each person gave a testimony about how I had affected their lives. They said so many nice things, it was hard to take it all in.

Krystal, said that she and Renee had appreciated my encouragement when we sang with Eloise Laws in Miami. After I became a Christian, they had watched my life. "I know God is using you," Krystal said. "And you have had a real influence on my life. I'm happy to be a part of your life, and to know that you are a friend." *

---

* Krystal and Renee turned to Jesus Christ. Several months before my going away party, both received baptism at the Greater Refuge Temple.

Yvonne told about some of the things we'd enjoyed together before I became a Christian, such as going to night clubs. She concluded by saying, "Lala, in so many ways we are the same. We look much alike, we talk alike, and we sing alike. We were together in the world, and now we're growing in the Lord together. There are many parallels in our life." Until then she had been laughing and telling a lot of funny stories. Then she paused, wiped her eyes and said, "I hate to lose you and to see you go off, but I know God has called you, and you have to go. You'll always be in my heart."

Pastor Murray asked to say something before he closed our party with prayer. "Ullanda, I don't know what God has in store for you," he said, "but I know God is going to use you mightily. Be faithful, and whatever He calls you to do, do it. I know I'm going to read about you somewhere or hear about you again."

Then we all held hands and Pastor Murray led us in a heart-felt prayer that brought tears to our eyes. With those beautiful words, we parted.

Two days later, I left for Uchee Pines.

• • •

I moved to Uchee Pines in October of 1986 and stayed until July of the following year. It was exactly what I needed for it helped me truly break with my old life. In that caring atmosphere, I found peace. More fervently than ever before, I studied the Bible and learned so much about the Christian faith. I also learned how to do medical missionary work and preventive medicine techniques.

For the entire period I stayed at Uchee Pines, residual checks continued to flood in, so money was no problem. I took on the music ministry at the school, urging the choir to work hard so we could sing Handel's "Hallelujah Chorus." This was quite a challenge because many of the members had not sung in a choir before and knew little about music. I sought out those who had good voices and taught them as much as I could within a short period of time. And when we performed, I was proud of them.

Yes, Uchee Pines stands out as a special time in my life because it provided the time and place to make a transition. I mended after the emotional pain of breaking up with Tyrone. Slowly I moved away from the temptation of needing jewels and furs. They would never again become a false god in my life.

In my thinking, I had left the jingle business, and now I prayed about a new direction for my life. Although I had no impelling vision, I felt drawn to take up midwifery. I met a number of midwives who came through Uchee Pines for brief periods. Without exception, each one told me how much she loved and valued her work. Several of them suggested I apply for the midwifery course at Living Springs in upstate New York. That seemed the next step for me. Friends back in New York wrote or called often. Tyrone called and sent me pictures. Once he suggested, "Let's get married and move to California." Yvonne called and told me, "Tyrone was in church again this Sabbath. Maybe he's really changing."

I prayed, "Lord, is this right? Is this what you want from me?" I still had deep feelings for Tyrone, and yet I couldn't feel that God was telling me to say yes and go back to him.

Other complications revolved around calls to lure me back into the business. One such call came from a producer of the music for the *Bill Cosby Show,* who invited me to return to New York and sing the theme for a new Black sitcom, *A Different World.* If my career had still been important to me, it could have been a marvelous opportunity. But I wasn't even tempted.

While I was growing and trying to discern God's will for my future, I often thought about marriage. The longer I stayed away from Tyrone, the more convinced I was that I had done the right thing in leaving him. It took several months, but I surrendered my dream of marriage to Tyrone. Yet I still wanted to be married someday.

Probably every day I prayed about a husband. Some people can live their lives without needing to share themselves with another significant person. I'm not that way. I need another person around me. "Lord, prepare me to be a virtuous woman," I prayed, "but send me a husband soon because it's difficult for me to be out here alone at Uchee Pines. I am Your child, and for You I left the lure of the world and everything that would turn me in the wrong direction. But, God, I really need a mate."

One night I had a vivid dream, so real I knew God was speaking to me. In this dream I married a man, but I couldn't see his face. However, many of those present, especially the groom's family, were speaking French. My family didn't meet his family until the wedding. When I awakened, the most powerful aspect that remained with me was that my husband's family was speaking French. I didn't know anyone who spoke French!

The next afternoon found me sitting alone in the Uchee Pines cafeteria after lunch. I was thinking about my dream and trying to understand its message. Just then I looked up and saw a handsome Black man walk into the nearly empty room. After getting his food, he came over and asked, "May I sit next to you?"

"Of course."

He told me his name was Vincent Davis and that he was visiting from New York, had enrolled in a premed program, and wanted to spend a little time at Uchee Pines to learn more about nutrition. We had a lovely chat together. Still pondering the dream, I thought, *wouldn't it be something if Vincent turned out to be the man I married. We continued to talk, and he said something that grabbed my attention.*

". . . happened when I was living in Paris. And by the way, I still miss that city."

"Paris? You actually lived there?"

"Why yes—"

"And you speak French?"

"Yes, I do. Why?"

"Oh, just asking," I said calmly, but inside my heart was racing. *Oh God, he seems so nice. Is this the man You want me to marry?*

I hoped God was going to say yes.

• • •

During the three-month period Vincent stayed at Uchee

Pines, he spent most of his free time with me and another new friend named Lance Williams. Vincent was so likable and just plain sweet. Everybody on campus loved him and thought he was the dearest person.

I kept asking, "God, is it possible that you have sent Vincent to me? I like him very much, but that's not enough. If he is the man, he must be as committed to You as I am. If he is the one in the dream, help me to know." I was confused because there was another young man at Uchee Pines whom I thought could be God's will for me. He was a committed Christian, attractive, very tall, and musically inclined. But once I had the dream and then met Vincent, I blocked any chance for a relationship to develop between us.

During the next three months, while Vincent was at Uchee Pines, we became very good friends. When he returned to New York he asked if we could keep in touch. We did, and grew even closer. When I had to go back to New York for some business, I let Vincent know I was coming. It was in New York City that he first told me that he loved me. He also said that he loved children and wanted to have a house full of them.

I returned to Uchee Pines but we continued our friendship. By now it had grown far beyond mere friendship. I didn't want to lose him—but I knew I had to tell him the truth, that I couldn't bear children. But I couldn't bring myself to face it and the possibility of losing him.

Some weeks later I was back in New York City for a friend's wedding, and knew I couldn't put it off any longer. And so I told him.

"Why didn't you tell me before?" he asked. "All this time I've been talking about our having children and you haven't said anything."

My tears flowed so hard that I couldn't talk. My worst nightmare had come true. *Oh, God*, I said, *How can he just walk away from me now? I thought everything was perfect, and now he doesn't want me.*

We talked for a long, long time and smoothed things over before we parted. But I knew I had lost him for good.

The hurt continued for a long time.

• • •

After that I closed myself off even though Vincent continued to write to me. In essence the messages were, "Ullanda, I can't marry you, but I do love you."

As he continued to write, my spirits rose. Yet no matter how much we talked, the bottom line for him was if I couldn't have kids, marriage wasn't possible. He wasn't going to change.

I felt as if I faced the end of my life. *I'll be single for the rest of my life*, I thought. *I can't have kids, and most men want children.* I felt terrible and was furious with God for what had happened to me.

Slowly I started to emerge from my pain. I asked God's forgiveness for being so angry. God's comfort engulfed me, and slowly a peace came into my heart. "I'm yours, God. Whether I'm married or not, You are with me."

From Uchee Pines, I moved back to New York, then to Paris to an SDA medical missionary institute. I felt that, by getting totally away from everyone I knew, it would be easier to get past Vincent's rejection and my pain. I stayed six weeks. During that time, I did a lot of soul searching and praying for God's help.

By the time I returned, inner healing had taken place. I was over my anger, my pain, and my feelings for Vincent.

Chapter 24

. . . .

*B*ack to New York," I sighed.

I had mixed emotions about returning, but where else should I go until I had directions from God?

When I returned in July of 1987, I assumed I would stay only a few weeks at most, so I stayed with Judy and Todd Glasco for a while. Then I moved in with a girlfriend named Gwen Conley. She had a nice, small apartment in Brooklyn Heights. Gwen was also in the jingle business and had become active in our Friday night Bible studies. She was Baptist, and I was an Adventist. Because we were friends and both Christians, I found exactly the atmosphere I needed as I continued to go through my healing process. The longer I stayed, the more the healing took place inside me.

Gradually I released my emotional tie to Vincent. I began to accept that I had made foolish decisions in the past, but they were part of the past, and I could do nothing to change them. Gradually, I accepted myself and my decisions, and finally I forgave myself. During those weeks, Gwen listened. And she cared.

I applied to the midwifery school at Living Springs, a school in upstate New York, but there was no place for me to stay while I took the course. Months later, I still didn't know what I would be doing as I still had no place to live at Living Springs. I fasted and prayed. I read the Bible. I begged God for guidance. But I got no strong impression. I didn't know what to do. Then circumstances convinced me that God had closed the door to midwifery for me.

I had a new realization that I didn't know what to do except to wait on God. I had given my life for God's service. Now it was God's problem and not mine. Since the door of midwifery had closed, I could only think of one other possibility for work. I'd prayed for guidance but hadn't gotten a clear direction from God as to what to do next. So I did the only thing left for me—I would return to singing jingles.

"Unless you show me a different way, God," I said, "this is the only kind of work I know."

• • •

It wasn't easy for me to try to enter the jingle world after having said goodbye. Only a year earlier I'd told everyone, "I'm leaving the business." Now I had come back because I needed the work. To their credit, not one person sneered or said, "Hey, I told you so."

Producers and contractors began to call me. "It's wonderful to have you back," they said. Immediately I got several jingles for Saab, which was a national spot, and it paid big money.

My first big problem had been a place to live and my solution was only temporary. Staying with Gwen was fine for a while, but it wouldn't work on any long-term basis. When Gwen left every morning, she took her press kit and pictures and went to various agencies where she left packets. The idea was that if they liked what they saw, they would hire her to do on-camera commercials. (My field was audio, but she liked video.)

Gwen often urged, "Ullanda, get your pictures done and work up a bio. Make up a press kit and go with me. If you're going to stay in the business, you need to move into on-camera television spots. And you do that by passing out your résumé and letting people see you."

"No, I'm fine," I kept telling her. "I'm waiting on the Lord to find out what I'm supposed to do." She didn't understand, and I couldn't blame her. Even though I had no sense of direction from God, I couldn't believe that I'd sing jingles indefinitely. Each morning after Gwen left, I stayed in the apartment and prayed, quite literally, for hours. All through the day, when I wasn't praying for guidance, I memorized portions of the Bible such as Psalm 91 and Revelation 14.

My money was running low and to make the living situation more urgent, Gwen's brother needed to move in with her. That meant I had to get out. But where was I to go?

And I had another problem. I wondered if singing jingles was right for me? If God led me this way, why didn't I enjoy my work the way I had in the past? More and more I began to listen to the words I sang as I pitched various products through the jingles. Some products I could never advertise again. True, I wasn't singing for any of those right now, but it would be only a matter of time until that came up. Once I started turning down work, I'd be on the way out of the business. Jingle singers sing when asked. If they say no, they stop getting asked.

Poor Gwen finally lost her patience with me for not going out and trying to get more work. To her, praying was right, but she felt I needed to take action as well. She knew I had all but exhausted my savings and I had no money coming in. One afternoon when she came back to the apartment, she stared at me in surprise, "Ullanda, you're still praying? Don't you think you need to do more than pray? You need to put some feet on those prayers."

Despite Gwen, I stayed in the apartment and prayed.

No answer came.

Finally I called the union to notify them that I was going back into the business, and I needed to activate my membership in the Screen Actors Guild (SAG). "Ullanda," the woman said. "I'm so glad you called. I've been trying to find you for months."

"Oh? Why?" I asked.

"Your residual checks. I've been putting them in escrow because I didn't know where to send them."

"We had a big stack of checks here for you and we didn't know what to do with them." She put me on hold while she added up the total—slightly over $8,000.

"I can't believe it!" I yelled after I hung up. "Lord, this is incredible! Here I am thinking I'm broke and wondering what I'm going to do and where I'm going to live! And, God, you've already provided."

The total wasn't a lot of money, but it was money. At first

Gwen couldn't believe it. Then she began to laugh. "This surely is something. Here I am walking the street, getting tired, killing myself to get jobs, and all you do is sit at home and pray, and God sends you money."

"Gwen, that's why you have to depend on the Lord. There's nothing you can do on your own strength. You've got to trust God, and He'll provide."

Two days later, I found a great apartment. That very day I gave the landlord a month's rent and another month's deposit. I felt so good knowing that I had my own place again. And not just any place. I had rented one in Brooklyn Heights, an incredibly beautiful, two-story flat with a patio on the top floor. Through the windows in the living room I could see the East River and the Statue of Liberty. This dream place had three fireplaces. It even had two separate entrances.

Immediately after moving in, I had the place remodeled. Then I sold the furniture that Dennis had been keeping for me and bought everything new.

Although I didn't realize it then, God still had lessons to teach me. I'm embarrassed to confess how foolishly I spent money. It seems odd as I look back that I had surrendered my jewelry and clothes, but I was still caught up in wanting fine things. Not to imply that a Christian can't have nice things, but God had been dealing with me. Because I was back in the jingle business again, I thought money would come in as it had in the past. So I spent money as easily and freely as I used to.

I got a loan from the credit union to take care of the renovating expenses and it still didn't occur to me that I was being foolish. I had a beautiful place to live in an area I loved, and all I had to do was wait for more sessions to come in. People liked me and called me to sing.

After spending $20,000 on redoing my apartment, I was ready to show it off. By then I was working part-time as director for the choir at New Hope Seventh-day Adventist Church. I invited the pastor, Abraham Jules, as well as the members of the choir and other church friends to bless the apartment. Pastor Clement Murray from Ephesus Church also joined us. We had a delightful time of praise and worship. Then Pastor Jules led us in a ceremony where he blessed the apartment.

My life had come full circle since my conversion. Money flowed in. I loved being part of New Hope Church, and I had made many new friends.

Everything was going to be easy and simple.

How little I knew what lay ahead.

Chapter 25

• • • • • • • • • • • • • • • • • • •

Jingle sessions were coming in, and my friends had welcomed me back. Most important, I was working in the church too. In that same year of 1988, I assisted the pastor in a crusade in Harlem by singing as the soloist. *This is just perfect,* I thought. *I'm working for the Lord at the church, and I support myself by singing. This couldn't be better.*

Then everything fell apart.

SAG went on strike. That included jingle singers. All of a sudden I wouldn't have a job anymore.

My landlord called when he heard about the strike, and I explained my situation to him. He was very kind. "Tough times happen to all of us," he said. "We'll work with you."

I fell on my knees, filled with remorse at the money I'd spent and the debts I owed. "Lord, I don't understand what You're trying to do with me. I realize now that I'm still caught up in wanting fancy things and spending a lot of money. I was wrong and very foolish, I can see that now. I know You want to deliver me from that, but please I need a place to live. Don't take this apartment from me."

A month later the landlord called again. "Ullanda, we've got problems," he began. He explained that investments which he and his wife had made were not bringing in the expected money. They were going to have to sell the apartment.

"I can't afford to buy it," I said, "so that means I need to move out."

They were kind and told me that, because of my deposit, I

could stay another month. I thanked them for being so kind, but that gave me only a temporary answer. I had only 30 days before I would have to move out.

For the next few days my emotions fluctuated between tears and despair. Tears flowed because I'd put $20,000 into renovating the apartment. Of that amount, I had borrowed $12,000. Even worse, I would get nothing back from the upgrading I had done. *Oh, God, I'm in a bigger mess than I was in when I moved back to New York. Now what am I going to do? Where am I going to live? How am I going to make a living? This strike can go on for months.* I contacted my friends and asked them to pray for me. A few days later, a lovely woman from the church, Janet Holmes, called and said, "I think I have a solution for you."

I sighed with relief, ready for any kind of help. "What do you think I could do?"

"You know Sylvia Davis in the church, don't you? She has a big apartment in Harlem, and she has two empty rooms. I'm sure she'll rent one to you with no problem. A long time ago I lived there myself."

"In Harlem?" I was afraid to live there, and even hated to visit the area.

"Ullanda, what else are you going to do? You have nowhere else to go, and you're going to have to make a decision."

"OK," I said, "I'll talk to her." Silently I prayed, *Lord, you're trying to humble me, and that's fine, but do you have to send me to Harlem?*

So I talked to Sylvia Davis and she was delighted to have me. "My husband has rheumatoid arthritis, and he's in a wheelchair. If you don't mind living with us, it's no problem, and we'll love to have you." As I listened to her, I felt worse. *God, I'm going to be living in this house in Harlem with people old enough to be my parents. You're putting me under their roof and I suppose that means I'll have to do whatever they say and abide by their rules, and have them monitoring everything I do. Oh, Lord, why are you putting me through this?*

Mrs. Davis gave me her address and the next day I went to see her home. When I got to the building I said, "Lord, this cannot be Your will."

I stared at a partially demolished building. "Nobody could

live in such a terrible place," I said aloud. The windows on the lower levels had been broken out. Even from the outside, I could see fire and water damage all over the inside. (I learned later that the Dance Theatre of Harlem had been across the street, and they also owned the apartment building. They wanted to take over the building to house their students. Sylvia was the only tenant who refused to move out, because her husband was in a wheelchair. She searched for another place, but she could find nothing they could afford that allowed easy access for her husband's wheelchair. The Dance Theatre took her to court and lost. A short time afterward—whether arson or accident never came to light—the building caught on fire. The flames gutted the apartments; the water-damaged walls and ruined ceilings made it impossible to renovate. However, the fire didn't affect the Davis's apartment that much. Despite the extensive damage to the building, she still refused to move from her fifth-floor apartment. They were the only tenants who chose to stay.)

As I surveyed the partially destroyed building, I wanted to turn and flee. But I couldn't. Slowly, reluctantly, I walked to the front door, all the while hoping I had the wrong place. Then I saw the Davis' name plate. I choked back tears as I pressed the doorbell.

"Hi, Ullanda, come on up," came Sylvia Davis's friendly voice.

As I started toward the fifth floor, I stared at the debris that filled the hallways. I shuddered. I couldn't think of a worse place to live. *God, I'm supposed to live here? How can I? There'll be rats and roaches and who knows what else. Oh God, please help me.*

Somehow I forced myself to knock. Mrs. Davis opened the door, and immediately I entered a new world. I saw a spacious, clean, and tastefully decorated apartment.

"What a lovely, lovely place," I said in amazement.

"It's home to us," Sylvia said and showed me a comfortably large room. "Whatever you want to give me a month to cover your room and board is fine." She made it clear that she wasn't laying down any rules, and I could come and go as I pleased.

OK, God, I prayed, as I stared at the clean, airy room, *inside it's not that bad, but I still don't like it. Is this a needed lesson for me? Do I still need to be humbled?* Even as I asked, I knew that I did. I had been so used to the fancy and the expensive. Now I was going to live in a place I wouldn't want my friends to see.

As much as I hated the idea, I knew this was where God wanted me. I had been so foolish with money, and now I was learning my lesson the hard way.

• • •

By September of 1989, I sensed that I had found God's direction for my life. Music was my career and my ministry. God had given the gift of singing. Despite the on-going SAG strike, doors had begun to open for me to sing for evangelistic crusades. The more I accepted such opportunities, the more natural it felt.

God, I prayed, *this is the way You want me to go, isn't it? To sing in churches and evangelistic crusades?* No distinct answer came, yet I felt at peace. *If God is leading me,* I reasoned, *the invitations will continue to come.*

One day I received a phone call from Lionel and Pat Martell in Alabama. Lionel, then a student at Oakwood College in Huntsville, was preparing for the ministry. I'd known about the school for a couple of years, as the members of a prominent singing group, Take Six, had graduated from there. So had Clifton Davis, the singer and star of the popular TV sitcom, *Amen.*

"Ullanda, if you really want to get into singing in crusades and that kind of thing," Lionel said, "come down here. Pat and I will do what we can to open doors. I'll introduce you to the president of the college and to a lot of pastors. I'm sure we can help you set up concerts."

"Do come," Pat urged. "We want to help." They asked me to stay with them and the more I prayed about it, the better I felt about going. I had grown tired of living in New York. And I never lost my desire to get out of Harlem. I arranged to visit the Martells for a weekend.

As it turned out, I stayed away from New York for three months.

During those weeks in Alabama, I assumed I'd return to New York so I kept sending my rent payment. When I wasn't involved in crusades or invited for other singing dates, I attended the campus church where Lionel Martell assisted the senior pastor. Often

I sang in their services. This experience gave me a lot of exposure because church leaders visited the college, worshiped at the church, and heard me sing. But most of the exposure came through the church's weekly radio program.

"Got good news for you," Pat said one day. "Know who's coming here? Pastor Robinson, that's who."

"Really?" I felt excited. Reginald Robinson was the associate speaker for a TV program called *Breath of Life*, probably the most significant ethnic telecast done by the SDA church. BET carried the half-hour program on their cable channel.

"He's going to preach during the week at Oakwood College," Lionel said.

"If you can be heard by the *Breath of Life*," Pat said, "they'll love you and want you to sing regularly for them. It would be just exactly the kind of ministry we've been talking about." She didn't need to tell me that *Breath of Life* held evangelistic crusades all over the world. The Martells arranged for me to sing one night during their scheduled week of prayer. Unfortunately for me, Pastor Robinson didn't speak that night. On that particular evening, the featured speaker was Elder Robert Folkenberg.

"That's wonderful," I said and meant it. If God wanted Pastor Robinson to hear me, that would work out. I had never met Elder Folkenberg, but I knew he was a prominent speaker. (He has since become SDA General Conference president.) He was gracious to me, and I thoroughly enjoyed meeting him and hearing him speak.

Then no more invitations came. Not one. It seemed as if one day all the doors just closed, and I didn't know why. "What do I do now?" I asked the Lord. I had to do something soon.

Once again, just before I got desperate, Beverly Jenkins called from Nashville. "Do you remember me? Yvonne introduced us over the phone a couple of years ago. We were trying to get a singing group together."

"Oh, yes, of course I remember. How are you?"

"I'm fine. I understand you're in Huntsville. That's only about an hour and a half from Nashville. Why don't you come over and pay me a visit?"

While I was hesitating, not sure if I ought to go, she said,

"Do come. You can stay at my apartment, and it's yours for a week or two or three, no problem. Maybe I can introduce you around and we'll see what happens."

"I'd like that," I said, pleased to have any kind of invitation. "I'll come and visit you."

The following week I went to Nashville and Beverly graciously opened her place for me. Just about the time I came, there was some kind of musical convention in town. She urged me to attend with her and I did.

Once I got there, Beverly offered me another suggestion. "Why don't you make your own album? You really need to commit yourself to a record company."

"I don't know," I answered, "I'm not really interested in recording right now. Too much of a hassle, and I'm really trying to get out of the scene of recording anyway."

"No, no, Ullanda. Listen to me. You really need to put together a press kit, and print business cards, have pictures made, and write up your bio. The whole bit."

"I already have my bio done. Pat and I had it done in Huntsville."

"That's a start," she said, "but it's not enough. You need to have pictures and put together a showcase.* Also, I want to introduce you to some musicians here in Nashville that are excellent."

"Look, I don't know if this is right."

"Do you know it's wrong? Think about it. You want people to know about you and what you're doing, don't you? Sometimes you have to tell them where you are before they can find you." We talked about this for quite a long time before I was finally able to agree.

A few days later, Beverly invited me to her mother's house after church. On our way to the house, Beverly said, "Oh, by the way, I've invited Mervyn Warren as well."

"You invited *who?*" Mervyn is the lead singer and head producer for Take Six. "I didn't realize you knew him."

"Know him? Why, the members of Take Six go to our church."

---

* *Showcase* is a mini-concert set up for producers and people in the music business. They come to see the performer live, and if they like what they see, it can lead to a recording contract.

"Really?" This was another surprise. "You've never mentioned it before."

"Yeah, I suppose not. You see, to me they're kids, local talent. I went to school with them, so it's no big deal to invite Mervyn and the others over."

"Beverly, they're the hottest thing going right now. No matter whether it's secular, jazz, or pop. Why, they're getting awards for every category."

"Yeah, of course I know." She laughed as if this was no big thing for her. "Oh, and I've also invited Brian Jones."

"You've really been at work," I said. Brian Jones was a pianist with an excellent reputation.

"I invited them so you can meet and talk with them, and see what ideas they come up with. They're the kind of people who like to help others get going."

Once I arrived, I realized that it was an open house and people milled around everywhere. A grand piano sat in the middle of the living room.

I liked Mervyn immediately. He was quiet and soft spoken with a warm, engaging smile. His group was at the top of the charts, yet no one would know it from the down-to-earth way he behaved. As we talked about the music business I thought, *Wow, this guy is awfully nice to be involved in Take Six. He could be a star and be a demanding personality, but he's warm, friendly, and so accommodating.*

It surprised me most when Brian said, "I've never met a real jingle singer before. We're all honored to meet you. You still sing. Right?"

"Oh, yes. That's what I feel God has called me to do."

We continued to talk, and then eventually Beverly came over and said, "You need to put together a showcase, Ullanda. That's why I brought Brian. He'll help you do it."

"Of course," Brian said. "When Beverly told me what you had in mind, I was glad to say yes. Now that I've met you, I'm even more pleased to do what I can."

I felt very grateful to Beverly for caring that much.

Maybe this is where things turn around for me.

Perhaps God was leading me to Nashville and a recording career.

Chapter 26

. . . .

My new friends in Nashville did everything they could to help me. No matter what happened, I decided, I would always be thankful for these unselfish, caring people who took me, a stranger, and accepted me as a friend.

A few days after our initial meeting, Brian Jones sat down with Beverly Jenkins and me to work on the showcase. My first concern was the cost factor. Take Six's manager, Gail Hamilton, volunteered her time and expertise and taught us exactly how to go about setting up everything. She even booked the studio for me and handled dozens of details I hadn't considered. Brian and I spoke with Roland Gresham, a highly gifted guitarist, who also agreed to perform with me on the showcase.

We put together a list of the different companies and the names of their representatives and sent them invitations. By the time we started rehearsals we had a five-piece band that consisted of drums, bass guitar, flute, keyboard, and electric guitar. We decided to hire three background singers. One of them was Kim Fleming, a pop artist who had moved into the Christian field. Kim was then working with Amy Grant. I'd never met Kim, but Beverly knew her and asked her to sing back-up.

"I'd love to sing with you," Kim said when we finally met. "I've always hoped I'd have a chance to meet you. I'm a background vocalist too and for years it seemed as if every time I read an album label, I came across your name."

Later both of us laughed about the way she'd dressed for the meeting. So that she wouldn't feel out of place, Kim wore an impressive two-piece black suit, perfectly matching jewelry, and exquisite make-up, all amplifying her short, black hair and lovely complexion. Wearing her very best, she met a plainly dressed woman who wore no make-up or jewelry.

After we got to know each other better, she told me her first reaction was to ask herself, *Can this be Ullanda McCullough?* She had assumed I would come in wearing furs and diamonds and clothes right out of a couturier's salon. When she told me this, she added, "But you know, it showed me that you really were converted. You didn't need all of that. You were just yourself." Her words flabbergasted me. I didn't think that my wearing or not wearing jewelry or furs had been any big deal to the way Christians perceived me. I had stopped wearing them because it had become a barrier between God and me. Certainly, I had never intended this to tell others how to dress. And she did understand that.

I was delighted that Kim would sing background for my showcase. She also contacted two other female vocalists who did jingles and background vocals for artists such as Larnelle Harris to sing for us.

We sent hundreds of invitations to the showcase, rented a beautiful studio, paid a lot of money for the clothes, the band, and rehearsal space. "But it will be worth all the investment," Beverly kept saying. "Once they meet you, those producers will love you."

Five days before the showcase, we discovered that we had a problem. Unknowingly, we had booked the showcase for the same night as an annual music festival in Nashville. All the record company people go to it in their search for new talent.

Not one record executive showed up for my showcase.

Actually one man did come, a representative of the William Morris Agency. He came only because Valerie Simpson had personally asked him. However, I never heard from him.

Church members came. And the pastor of the church I attended. And a handful of friends. About 70 altogether, but nobody from the record companies. The lack of turnout crushed me.

Oh, God, I tried so hard. We all worked on this and gave it our best. All this time, energy, and money, and all for nothing. I tried to hide my disappointment from my friends, but I couldn't hide it from myself or from God. Money had come in from jingle residuals and I had spent more than half of it to put on the showcase. *What a waste,* I kept thinking. I didn't know what else to do but pray. It took a couple of days, but I finally pulled out of my despair. I was able to give it to God, sincerely thinking, *Unless it's God's time for you, Ullanda, you may as well forget it. No matter how much energy you put into something, if God is not in it, it's not going to work.*

But everything wasn't lost. Kim Fleming spread the word that I was a Christian singer, who was going to be in Nashville for a few weeks, and wanted to work. I got several calls to do sessions and back-up on Christian labels. At that time a lot of Christians were recording in Nashville.

Bob Bailey, who wrote the song, "Stand,"—a fine singer and songwriter himself—attended the showcase. He also helped to spread the word about me. Because of Bob and Kim, I got to sing on one of Al Green's Christian albums. When the Benson company signed Clifton Davis, I sang on his album as well.

Wintley Phipps still called me to work with him occasionally. I wasn't as busy as I needed to be, but enough work came in to encourage me. I could probably make enough to support myself. By this time I realized I wouldn't return to Harlem. I called Mrs. Davis and explained my situation. Being the lovely lady she is, she understood. I then took an apartment in Nashville. *God knows where I am,* I reminded myself.

Then a Nashville pastor invited me to sing one night for an evangelistic meeting. That invitation thrilled me because I felt so at home singing under those circumstances. He told me, "Evangelist E. E. Cleveland is preaching the same day you'll be singing. Once he hears you sing, I know he'll hire you."

I thanked him for his support and enthusiasm and prayed for God's will to be done.

During the service, I sang, "He Is Able." After I finished, Pastor E. E. Cleveland paused as he stepped up to the pulpit to preach, and said to me, "Young lady, you're hired."

"Oh, thank you," I said, excited that it had happened just

that way.

The evangelistic meetings would last six weeks. For six weeks at least, I wouldn't need to worry about other work coming in. The pastor who coordinated the crusade asked me if I'd be interested in writing and producing jingles for the meetings. The Lord helped me write and then sing a catchy little jingle to play on the air as part of the announcement for the crusade. E. E. Cleveland liked them.

It was an inspirational and exciting six weeks. One night Take Six came to sing. I couldn't believe how wonderful those days were. On another night, Wintley Phipps appeared on the program and ministered in song.

To my surprise, they had another guest preacher in the Cleveland Crusade, Pastor Reginald Robinson from *Breath of Life*. Though based in southern California, the *Breath of Life* quartet had decided to fly to Nashville to sing one night, and he came with them.

In the workers' meeting before the evening service, Reginald Robinson was present, and E. E. Cleveland asked me to pray for God's blessings in the meetings. As I started to pray, I felt greatly burdened for those who had not experienced the love of God in their hearts. I don't remember how long I prayed or what I said, but the words poured out from deep inside. I began to cry as I called on the Lord.

When the meeting concluded, Pastor Robinson started talking to me. I liked his manners and his genuine warmth. He said to me, "Young woman, you really know how to pray."

"I was praying to the Lord," I said, flustered at the compliment. "I just prayed what was on my heart."

"And it touched me," he said. "Besides, I've wanted to meet you. For some time now I've been hearing about you."

"Really? From whom?"

"Your name comes up often in the SDA Church. Most recently, Pastor Wintley Phipps told me about you. I understand that you were in the music world and you came out of it. Pastor Phipps baptized you."

"Oh, yes, that's true," I said. "And now I'm using my talent to sing for the Lord."

"Ullanda, now that you're singing gospel music, I want you to work for me."

"You do?" I remembered that months earlier when I'd lived with the Martells I'd longed for him to hear me sing, and it hadn't worked out. Now without my having to do anything but pray, he came to me.

"I've scheduled a crusade in Detroit, and I want you to come and sing for me."

"Wonderful! Detroit is my home town."

"That makes it perfect, then, doesn't it? Wouldn't this be great for you to go back to Detroit and witness to your family and friends? It's going to be a wonderful meeting, and I know you'll be blessed."

He didn't settle anything, but he did take my phone number. Afterward I thought, *Oh, I've been through this kind of thing too often in New York. They say that they'll call, but they seldom do.* Based on my previous experience, I assumed that was the end of it.

"It's OK," I told God. "If You are in this, he'll call."

The E. E. Cleveland series concluded. Many responded to the Word and turned to Jesus Christ. I felt blessed to be a small part of it.

I'd been going through a lot of struggles and anxieties during those weeks. *What am I going to do after this? How can I continue to live?*

Just before the six weeks came to an end, Pastor Robinson did call, and he wanted me to work with him in Detroit as he had said. I thought this would be fine because I could keep my apartment and come back to Nashville when that was over. We would begin in October of 1990.

I was happy to be back in Detroit and to stay with Aunt Helen. But it felt strange to be in that house without having my grandparents around. It felt as if something was wrong with the house. They had always been so loving and supportive, and living in that large house had meant so much to me as a child. Every time I walked into the house, I felt the presence of my grandparents. And I missed them so much.

Then the meetings began. Twenty-seven of my relatives attended. One cousin, Marlon, turned to Jesus Christ and was baptized. Most of my family were already in the church, although we represented a variety of denominations such as Baptist, Pentecostal, Church of God in Christ, and Adventist. Most important to me, after my relatives listened to the sermons, they were finally able to understand that being an Adventist wasn't being part of a cult.

"Why, they preach the gospel just like our church does," one of my Aunts said.

"That's what I've been trying to tell you for a long time."

• • •

During the meetings I met a couple from California named Cliff and Freddie Harris. I had no way of knowing how important they would become in the next phase of my life.

Chapter 27

What a voice! You sounded just wonderful!" said a tall, good looking, middle-aged man. He came up to me after our opening night concert in Detroit and grabbed my hand. He was slightly over six feet tall, brown-skinned and well-dressed.

His voice held a happy tone and he wore a smile. "My name is Cliff Harris, and I want you to meet my wife, Freddie." She was very attractive, tall, and light-skinned. She wore a colorful dress that matched her outgoing personality. I was impressed that they were down-to-earth, genuinely nice people.

The opening night had been delightful. Wintley Phipps and I did a concert together and I told the story of my conversion to the audience. Pastor Robinson, too, had spoken to many hearts.

People came up to me after most concerts, and I always enjoyed chatting with them, but Cliff and Freddie were different. They had agreed to travel with the *Breath of Life* team to set up support groups for those who responded to the gospel.

They told me their fascinating story. Cliff, a drug addict before his conversion, had now become a helper of others who wanted freedom from drugs. As he testified one night before the audience, he had found Jesus Christ and dedicated his life to helping others do the same. A skilled mason, he continued to make his living in the building trade. It impressed me that Cliff and Freddie put their money and energy into their program called Drug Alternative Program (DAP).

We talked together often during the weeks of meetings.

Before they left to return to their home in southern California, they gave me their address and phone number. More than once Freddie said, "We want you to come out to California and do a concert for DAP."

"Sure, I'd love to," I said. I had at least one friend out there—a man I'd hoped to long-distance date, named Harrell. "Give me a call and let me know, and I'd be more than happy to do it."

Less than a week after the Detroit meetings ended, Freddie phoned. "If it's okay, we're setting up a concert for you here in Grand Terrace in December. Maybe we can help you line up other singing opportunities. You can stay at our home for a couple of months, or however long you want. Who knows what will open for you out here."

Cliff and Freddie lived in a lovely ranch house, nestled in a corner lot and surrounded by huge palms and a beautifully trimmed lawn. *Oh, Lord,* I whispered silently, *wouldn't it be nice to live in California? It's such a wonderful place, the weather is great, and the people I've met are nice.*

I already had a few other contacts and hoped that the DAP concert would open more doors for me. The concert for DAP went well and they received a number of donations from the audience.

During this same time, other than a few concerts and record dates, nothing much opened up for me in Nashville. I had nothing to take me back there. Since the Harrises had already invited me to stay in their home as long as I remained in southern California, I decided to accept their offer. I called several people I knew. Nothing happened immediately. It would take time, but I felt right about being in California. And I was willing to wait for God's direction.

After I'd been there a few weeks, Cliff came up with an idea so I could stay indefinitely. He offered me a position as a kind of supervisor-custodian in a house they had for those involved in DAP. "We're looking for someone to do this permanently," he said, "but if you'd live there and supervise them for six months or so, it would give you a place to operate from while you're making contacts. And it would give us time to find just the right person to live there permanently."

It seemed like a splendid opportunity for me, and I felt it was a way I could repay their kindness, so I agreed. The house had a private apartment, and Cliff loaned me a car. It should have worked well.

But it didn't.

Three men lived in the house at the time. They had kicked their drug habits and were in the process of returning to society. I really didn't understand such people. In the music business I had known those who used drugs of various kinds, but I had avoided them. These three men needed emotional support and empathy, and I just didn't know how to relate to them. I couldn't talk effectively with them or deal with their particular problems, so I tried to stay out of the house as much as possible. When I was there, I kept my apartment door locked. Looking back, it was a mistake for me to agree to live there. Almost from the first day I moved in I felt uncomfortable, but I'd never had any experience or training for the job. Naturally, my lack of adjustment disappointed Cliff. He expected me to oversee the home and be a kind of general caregiver for them, but I just couldn't do it. Freddie, Cliff, and I discussed this several times, and I think they believed they just needed to be patient with me and encourage me.

Then Cliff's patience ran out.

He called me into his office and said, "Ullanda, this arrangement isn't working. Maybe you should go back to Nashville."

In my misery, I had been praying for direction. But to return to Nashville didn't seem the right thing to do. Even without a house, I'd felt so at home in California. What did God want me to do?

"Cliff, I'm doing my best, and it's all I can do. If you can't accept what I'm doing, that's fine," I said. "I just can't do any better!" At the moment, I didn't feel good about it, and I was more disappointed in myself than he was. Maybe that's why I lashed out at him.

"I know God has a purpose for my being here in California," I added. "If you're not going to let the Lord use you to fulfill it, someone else will."

He was shocked and a few more words flew between us, but

we both recognized the inevitable decision—I would move out as soon as I could make other arrangements.

I held back the tears. It hurt to hear him talk about his disappointment in me and my lack of being able to help the men. Of course, he was right, but the words stung. As he talked, I kept thinking, *here I am doing them a favor, and they turn around after I agreed to it, and they have laid on expectations that are beyond me.* Even though I couldn't do the kind of job they wanted me to do, I felt I had done what I could.

After I left the office, I went back to my apartment and got ready to go to the Wednesday night prayer meeting at our church. By then I had calmed down and prayed about my attitude and what had taken place. I had been wrong. I had been ungrateful, too outspoken, and I had hurt Cliff's feelings. I didn't want to have any bad feelings toward him.

Ten minutes later, I went back to the office to let Cliff know I was leaving for church. His expression showed that he expected me to argue with him. "I'm going to church," I told him. "I'll be back later." Then I took a deep breath and added, "And thank you so much, Cliff."

Freddie felt badly about the whole thing. She and I were prayer partners. Wisely, she didn't try to get me to stay, but she did help me find a new place to live. Freddie suggested that I call a woman from the church who was able to let me have a place to rent.

My leaving was right for both Cliff and me. We had tried, and it hadn't worked. *But what now?* I asked myself. I didn't know what to do. A few residual checks were still coming in, accounting for most of my income. I did do occasional concerts, but I couldn't count on them. Several pastors had heard me, liked my singing, and called me for concerts. But I wasn't bringing in enough to do more than pay my rent and buy a few essentials.

I thought of going back to Nashville, but staying in California seemed right to me. Nashville had never really felt like home. I couldn't go back to New York and the life there. Maybe I still feared the temptation to return to the old lifestyle. And now I had found the place I knew I would be happy to live for the rest of my life. That meant I had to work hard to establish myself.

Harrell was still in the picture. I liked him, for he was a nice person and a fine Christian. He had grown up in an economically poor family, but became a medical doctor and was doing extremely well financially. He didn't talk about his money, but others told me he was a millionaire. His income didn't impress me. I had been around wealth before. I liked him and felt as if he and I could be good friends. I'd prayed for a sign and thought our relationship was God's will.

Then one evening Harrell said, "I like you, Ullanda, but, well, I date other women as well."

"That's fine. You go out with them," I said, "but I just don't operate that way. I pray you'll find the person God has for you, but do yourself a favor and don't marry someone out of your faith."

I didn't feel rejected. In fact, there may have been some relief for, looking back, I knew our breakup had been inevitable. We weren't right for each other.

An interesting sideline is that during the few weeks I had dated Harrell, I met a lot of people. They openly accepted me, and several of them treated me like a friend and spoke about my marrying the "millionaire boyfriend." Some of my New York friends got excited about this and pleaded, "Send us an invitation, and we'll fly out for the wedding."

When the word got around that Harrell and I were no longer dating, some of those nice, new friends began to treat me differently. Not outright snobbery, but their attitude had obviously changed. I felt as if I wasn't worth much to them now that I no longer dated a millionaire. Through this experience, I discovered my true friends. Those who pulled back had never really been my friends. I felt disappointed by their reaction. It also hurt that money made a difference in the way they treated me.

Money does strange things to people. I noticed that in the jingle business. When the wealthy and influential attended parties, they were the center of attention. It was as if having money made them more worthwhile, their jokes funnier, and their looks more glamorous. The real hurt came after a few people I had thought of as close friends no longer seemed to have time for me when I stopped dating Harrell.

I promised myself and God, "If I ever get into a position of having money again, I'm going to use it to help those in need.

And one thing, I'm not going to be around people who find me attractive because of the money. I want friends who are sincere."

● ● ●

At the end of 1990, just before Harrell and I decided not to continue to go out, I attended a prayer meeting at a church in Santa Ana. A few months later I realized that that night changed the direction of my life.

I sat by myself at the prayer meeting. After the service, Pastor Boger came up to me and introduced himself, and asked my name. When I told him, I also said I was visiting from Nashville.

"Why are you in town?"

"I'm here doing concerts, and I'm an Adventist so I decided I'd come to your church for your prayer meeting."

He asked a few questions and I told him about my work in jingles and background singing, and a few of the crusades I had done.

"Can you do a concert at my church in two weeks?" he asked.

"I could, but you've never heard me sing." His directness surprised me. "Why, you don't know anything about me. I could be anybody."

"No, I believe in you. I want you to come and do a concert at my church."

I said, "OK, I'd love to do a concert at your church."

When I told him my fee, he said, "No problem." And those few minutes after prayer meeting were destined to make a big difference in the rest of my life.

Chapter 28

· ·

I was excited when Pastor Boger invited me to sing at his church, but I needed more than the chance to minister through music. Something felt wrong with my life. Something was missing. I felt utterly depressed because I was tired of being alone. More and more, I felt lonely for the companion I didn't have. Some people can live alone and like it, but I needed another person—the right person.

This had been troubling me for a good long time, even as I knew Harrell wasn't the right man and we needed to break up. But I had met too many wrong men. I had grown tired of praying, tired of asking God to send me a lifelong companion. About the time that I was planning for the concert at Pastor Boger's church I became quite angry with God and demanded, "I need a husband, so send me one! Send me the man You have for me. In that dream You promised me a husband, so I want You to keep Your promise to me. If You don't send me a husband, that's it! I'm going back to New York, and I'm going to forget about any kind of ministry."

Through my early Christian teaching, I had been taught to tell God specifically what I wanted, and then give God a chance to give me that specific answer. I decided to do just that when I added, "God, please bring that man to the Santa Ana concert."

This painful episode took place two weeks before the concert. I was so disappointed because it seemed that all the available men in the church were playing the field. Maybe I was just too old fashioned, but I couldn't date that way.

The dream I had received at Uchee Pines never left me. No matter how down or discouraged I became, I had held on to that dream as a promise. "So where is that man?" I cried out to God. "You promised him. You showed me in a dream. Please, God, send that man."

Slowly the pain and depression left. The dream reminded me that God did have someone for me. I had grown impatient and demanding. "When, God?" I asked. "When do you send that right man into my life?"

I had peace that night.

But I didn't meet that new man I asked God to send me.

● ● ●

On the day of the concert, I prayed again, asking God to bring the right man to one of the two concerts I was doing that night.

The concerts went well, and I was in good voice. I gave my testimony and told them what God had done for my life. But I didn't meet the man I asked God to send, and it saddened me. Yet the people were very responsive and temporarily I forgot my pain and distress. It became clear to me that no matter how long I had to wait, I wasn't going to give up, and I wasn't going back to New York. However, the lonely ache inside didn't go away.

Afterward, people came up to visit with me. I met a woman named Plaida Valcin and her son, Frankie. They had appreciated the earlier service so much that they came back to the second concert, bringing friends with them. They were elated and thankful to God for the concert. "You have a gift," Plaida said, "a beautiful gift from God." Particularly she and the others told me how blessed they had been to hear the story of my conversion.

That night, it seemed Plaida was just another listener at the concert.

But, as I would learn, she was more than that.

● ● ●

In January, 1991, I was asked to sing with a concert at the Kansas Avenue Church in Riverside. They had booked a variety of singers and each of us did two numbers. My picture was prominently displayed along with those of the performers and that made me feel good. At least people were beginning to know who I was.

Because of Cliff and Freddie's friendship with Bill Tucker, I had tapes and videos to sell. The Harrises introduced me to Bill Tucker, president of *The Quiet Hour,* a television and radio ministry. Because of his relationship with DAP, Bill made a video for me on their set and he charged me nothing. From the video he made an audio cassette.

As people purchased materials from my table, they often said that they had been blessed by my singing. I never tired of hearing that my music had touched people's lives and felt thankful that I could do what I felt God had given me the talent to do. As a Christian, I was using my voice to advertise the one product I sincerely believed in—Jesus Christ. As the people milled around and chatted, I spotted Plaida Valcin and her son Frankie. I remembered her from our conversation at the Santa Ana Church. She stood quite a distance away, so I couldn't call to her. I saw another man with her—a very good-looking man— and assumed he was another son. A few minutes later Plaida turned toward me, so I waved at her. She didn't see me, however, but the man did. He waved back.

I laughed to myself and gave him a big smile. He didn't realize that he wasn't the one I intended to wave to. Several people were milling around my table, so it was several minutes before I could leave. When I finished with them, I went over and greeted Plaida.

The man who waved at me was clutching copies of my video and my audio tape under his arm. Apparently he had bought them from Cliff before I got to the table.

"Oh, hello Ullanda," Plaida said. "You remember my son, Frankie, don't you?"

"Yes, of course."

"And this is my other son, Patrick Innocent. I don't think you met him the other time, did you?"

"No, I didn't." As our eyes met, I felt an immense attraction to Patrick—something quite unlike anything I had experienced before. He was slightly over six feet tall, slender, and Ethiopianlooking with a dark-brown complexion. His fine features were clean shaven, and he had wavy hair.

"So, how are you doing?" Plaida asked. "I love to listen to you sing. We drove all the way from Anaheim just because we knew you would be singing."

We chatted a few minutes, and then Plaida turned and started to talk to someone else. Patrick, who had not moved or said anything other than hello, started talking to me. He was soft spoken and mannerly. We chatted several minutes and I realized he was easy to talk to.

Before they left, I learned that Patrick was a physical education teacher and a kinesiology* graduate student at Cal State University. Afterward, I couldn't believe I had asked so many personal questions, but I was curious to know about him. Without thinking about it, I assumed he must be married or have a girlfriend, yet I still thought he was nice and one of the most attractive men I had seen in a long, long time.

Just as they started to leave, Plaida asked, "Why don't you give me your number? We'd like to keep in touch. Maybe we could invite you to our home for dinner."

"Sure, I'd love to," I answered and gave her my phone number. I wondered if she would give it to Patrick as well.

I was living in Grand Terrace at a friend's house, about two-and-a-half hours' drive from where he lived in Northridge.

Two weeks later, I answered the phone and the voice at the other end said, "This is Patrick Innocent. Perhaps you remember me. Plaida introduced us at your concert."

Of course I knew him and was delighted he had called. I don't remember anything we said, but it was one of those fun conversations. He said a lot of clever, funny things and I laughed—more than I had laughed in a long time.

Just before we hung up, he said, "If you're ever at prayer meeting again in Anaheim, why don't you call me? Then I'll meet you there."

Wow, I thought, *he wants to go to prayer meeting with me. This is just the kind of man I want to know.* "OK, I'll do that."

---

*Study of anatomy in relation to human movement.

"Here's my number," he said. "Actually, it's my mom's number, and here's my number at my Cal State dorm." Before he hung up, I promised I'd call.

Because of other opportunities that opened up for me, it was two weeks before I was able to work out my schedule to go back to Anaheim. I decided I'd phone and let Patrick know that I just hadn't been able to get free. I called the first number, which was his mother's, and asked to speak to him.

"No Patrick Innocent here," the man's voice said with a kind of angry sigh.

"Is his mother there?"

"No, his mother doesn't live here."

"Thank you," I said, confused and disappointed. In that moment I realized then how much I was looking forward to seeing him again. I tried the number he'd given me for his dorm room but this time no one answered the phone. "Forget it, Ullanda," I told myself. "This guy played a joke on you." Somehow the whole thing felt strange. The person who had answered the first call sounded odd, even irritated, as if he had received other calls for Patrick at that number.

Two days later Patrick called me. "Hey, I've been waiting for you to call me, but you never did."

"Really?" I asked, trying to keep my voice level. "Actually I did call. When I couldn't get you, I asked for your *mother*. I asked for Mrs. Innocent, but the person who answered said your mother didn't live there."

"Oh, no wonder you're angry. I can hear it in your voice." He laughed. "Sorry, I didn't make that clear. Plaida really isn't my mother. She's my spiritual mom."

"It's still a strange situation to me," I said. "I called and the person said there was no Patrick Innocent there. He sounded a little rude—"

"Ullanda, I'm sorry. I'd better explain. You see, I'm going through a difficult time right now. That was probably her other son, Gibbs, who answered. He hasn't met you and didn't know who you were. You see, the family is trying to help me because I've been getting harassing phone calls. That's why they wouldn't give you any answers."

We kept talking. He explained that sometimes he forgot to turn on his answering machine in his dorm room. Soon we were laughing about the whole incident.

"When are you going to do another concert?" he asked. "I'd like to come to it."

"As a matter of fact, I'm doing another concert this weekend, but I don't think you'll be able to come."

"Why not?"

"Because it's in Orlando."

"That's no problem, I can come to Orlando."

"Not Orlando, California. Orlando, Florida."

"Tell me where it is and the time, and I'll be there."

"Come on, Patrick, give me a break. You men are all alike. You say these things, and then you don't come through." Convinced he was giving me a line, I became rather arrogant. "I'm sick of men who tell me one thing and do something else. I don't want to get involved again in any relationship like that. I want a man who is going to back up what he says."

"Fine. Because I'm telling you that if you tell me where it is, I will be there."

I thought, *This guy is too much.* "Furthermore," I said, "when I go to some city for a concert, I can't have a man following me across the country. It wouldn't look right. Besides, I don't really know you. Why, we've never even been out on a date."

"We could arrange that. Going on a date, I mean. How about it?"

"All right. Yes, all right, that will be fine with me."

"Why don't we do this?" he asked. "We've talked about going to the Wednesday night prayer meeting, so why don't we pray about it tonight? Both of us. Then I'll call you tomorrow. If God wants us to get together, we'll both feel right about it."

No man had ever approached me that way before. I could hardly believe his words. "Yes. Yes, that sounds wonderful," I managed to say.

After he hung up, I thought, *Hey, maybe this guy is all right. He wants to pray about going out with me. He wants me to go to a prayer meeting with him. He really is a Christian. Who knows? Maybe this might work out.*

That night I had the calmest, most peaceful sleep I had enjoyed in weeks. I didn't know what was going to happen, but Patrick and I were both asking God to show us His will.

"Oh, God," I said, as I drifted off to sleep, "how can we go wrong if we start out this way?"

• • •

"What's your answer?" Patrick asked when he called the next evening. "What did the Lord show you?"

"I feel impressed that we can at least go out together. That way, we'll begin to know what God wants in our lives. But it wouldn't be right for you to come to Orlando."

Patrick agreed and said he felt impressed that way too. "Why don't I pick you up tomorrow night?" he asked. "Let's go out to see if there's any chemistry, and if it's God's will."

We set up the date. No matter how excited I felt, I didn't want to get my hopes up. That had happened before, and I'd been shot down. So I called Yvonne in New York and said, "I met this guy, and he seems to be OK, but I'm not too sure. Would you please pray for me and for him?"

"Okay, Lala, I'll be praying for you and don't worry. God does have somebody special for you." Through the years since I had become a Christian, Yvonne and then later Pat Martell frequently encouraged me and prayed for the right man to come into my life.

"Just don't tell me again that this man is the one," I said. Yvonne, the perpetual optimist, had thought every man I dated was the one God had for me. "I want God's will. If this is the right man, it will work out."

"I'll be praying, Lala," she repeated.

• • •

Patrick and I had arranged to go out for dinner the next evening. He was late because of traffic, but he called to let me know. That he would be so considerate made him rise considerably in my estimation.

When he arrived in his Toyota 4x4 pickup, he walked in carrying a basket of red roses and a Valentine's Day card—the holiday was coming up that weekend. We went out to a lovely, quiet, vegetarian restaurant. I felt very comfortable with him—or as my New York friends used to say, we had good chemistry. As we talked, he shared his background with me. He was 33. After 15 years of marriage, he had gone through a divorce. In fact, the divorce had become final just a short time before we met. He had not wanted the divorce, and it meant giving up his two children, Joel and Thara, whom he loved dearly. But he did have visitation rights.

"Ullanda, I'm interested in finding out if the Lord has shown you what he has shown me," he said.

"What do you mean by that?"

"Pray. Ask God to show you what his will is for your life."

"I am. I do. Every day—"

"Ask him specifically what His will is for you."

"OK, I'll do that," I said, and did so that very evening. Patrick didn't know that sometimes when I'm in a public place or someone's home, and I feel impressed to pray, I go into the restroom so I can be alone. At the restaurant, I kept excusing myself to go to the ladies room because I wanted to pray. Patrick was talking like no one I had ever heard before and I just had to talk to God about him. He seemed too good to be true. "Oh, God," I said, "if this man is lying or not what he says he is, help me to know it. He seems nice, and I know he loves You. He's got a good job, and he's fun to be with, but don't let me get my hopes up and then get hurt again."

I didn't know that Patrick wondered if I had some kind of kidney disease or illness that kept me running to the ladies room.

One time when I returned to the table, he said, "Why don't we pray about our situation and see what God has in store for us? If God wants us to continue going together, we'll know it's the right thing."

"Yes, yes," I said, "that sounds right."

He took me home and parked in front of the house. "Before you go inside," he said, "would you like to have prayer right now, and a little worship?"

"Are you serious?" No man I dated had ever done that.

"Yes, I'm serious." He popped open the glove compartment, whipped out his Bible, and started to read one of the Psalms. As I listened, I was amazed. "Here is my favorite psalm," he said, and he began to quote it.

He quoted the Psalm in French.

I was holding my breath at one point, but when he finished, I asked "Do you speak French?" The question sounded stupid to my own ears.

"But of course I do. Don't you realize that I'm from Haiti? We speak French in Haiti."

I gasped.

"What's the matter?"

"I can't tell you right now," I said. "Maybe I can tell you later, but not now."

Chapter 29

· ·

*H*e speaks French. He speaks French. No matter how many times those words stirred inside my head, I could hardly believe it.

Oh, God, I prayed silently, *this time don't let me rush ahead of
You. Let me be sure.*

I'll never ever forget those minutes together when Patrick
brought me home. We sat in the cab of his pickup while he read
and quoted from the Psalms. Then we both prayed.

"Would you like to hear a song I wrote?" I asked him before
getting out of his Toyota. "It expresses what I feel right now."

"Of course," he said, "please do."

"It's called 'You Are My Joy,'" I said. We sat down on the
step and, as we looked into each other's eyes, I quietly sang him a
song that meant a lot to me.

"So beautiful," was all he said. Then he walked up to the door
and opened it for me. "Good night," he said and turned away.

As I lay in bed that night, I kept saying, "God, I can't believe
it. Can it possibly be that this is the French-speaking man from
my dream? Such a gentlemen and a Christian, and he fits everything in the dream! Can he really be the one?"

I had wanted to tell Patrick about my dream at Uchee Pines,
but I couldn't do it. The dream had been a powerful, encouraging
experience, but I had made the mistake of jumping to the con-
clusion that God had meant Vincent. This time I wanted no
mistake. But more than that, the dream had stayed with me,
often comforting me when I felt confused, alone, or depressed. If

I told Patrick now, would its impact evaporate? Besides, I reasoned that if God was bringing us together, we would both know it as we continued to date.

As I drifted off to sleep, I kept saying, "God, oh please let him be the man you have for me."

•   •   •

Patrick had insisted that I call him collect from Orlando. When I did, one of the first things he said was, "Well, have you prayed about us?"

"Sure, I'm praying, but I want to be sure. And I want you to be sure."

"That's fine," he said. "Keep praying." Before we hung up, he asked, "How are you getting home from the airport?"

When I told him I had arranged for a girlfriend to meet me, he asked if he could do it instead. I was thrilled that he wanted to, so I phoned my friend and told her she didn't have to come. When I got off the plane the next evening, Patrick was waiting for me. I had taken the red roses with me to Orlando and was still carrying them when I returned. He got my luggage and asked me to wait as he pulled up his 4x4. Inside, I saw a huge basket of flowers with a pink balloon heart. The card read, *Welcome Home*.

"You are too much," I cried. The basket of flowers was so large it wouldn't fit inside the truck with us. We had to put it in the back.

As we rode, I said, "Patrick, I can't believe all the kind things you're doing. Why are you being nice to me?"

"I asked you if the Lord had shown you anything. Has He?"

"Tell me more specifically what you mean."

He didn't answer, just drove in silence. At the house, he switched off the engine and turned toward me. "Ullanda," he said, "please tell me if the Lord has shown you anything."

"What are you trying to say to me?" I felt that he was making reference to possible marriage or something like that, but I needed to hear the words from him.

"Why don't we go somewhere and have dinner?" he said, instead of answering my question.

At the restaurant he said, "Ullanda, I don't know what the Lord has been showing you, and you're not willing to say right now. Fine. So I'll tell you where I am. I'm praying that you will be willing to marry me, because I know already that I want to live with you for the rest of my life."

I stared at him. "How can you even think such a thing? I've only known you a short time. Why, this is only our second date. Are you sure God is leading you?"

"I know this is God's will. I pray and I know it is right. Besides, I know already that I love you."

"How can you love me? You've just met me."

"I love the way you are in the Lord. You're a Christian, and I see that you're living according to the way the Lord would have you to. That's what I love about you. I love the Christ in you. I am totally serious that I want to spend the rest of my life with you."

"Excuse me," I said. I raced to the restroom, locked myself in a stall and prayed, "Oh, God, speak to me now. Is this right? Is this Your will? Is this what You want me to do?"

When I came back, he asked, "Do you have a problem with me? Or do you feel I'm not the right person? That you can't trust me?"

"It's none of that. I want to be sure. I've made mistakes before. And besides, I know God has called me to do His work through my singing."

"If you know that God has called you and that you are doing God's will, don't you also know that God will protect you from someone who isn't right for you? Are you saying you don't think you can trust me? That you have been too hurt in the past to trust me?"

"I'm still a little confused—"

"God is going to protect you and keep you from anybody who will cause you harm or try to lead you astray. Do you believe God is fighting your battles for you?"

"Of course I believe that, but—"

"Well, then you don't have to worry about me. I'm a Christian, and I love the Lord. I'm not here to hurt you or anything like that. God will protect you if I have any harmful ideas. I want you to trust me and to be honest with me."

The sincerity of his words, the vulnerability of his voice and face broke through my reserve and my guard came down. I decided to tell him everything! "Let me tell you," I began, for a long time I've been praying for a husband." Finally I told him about begging God to bring that very man into my life that night. "Specifically, I wanted God to send the man to me the night of the Santa Ana concert. And nothing happened, Patrick. I was so sure God would answer, but it didn't happen. And I've been a little confused since then."

"God did answer your prayer, Ullanda. I was at the concert in December."

"No, you weren't."

"I was there."

"I didn't see you."

"I know, but I was there with Plaida and Frankie."

"Why didn't you come up and introduce yourself?"

"I had broken my arm at school during one of the football games." He laughed self-consciously. "When I saw and heard you, you really impressed me. I felt I had to meet you and get to know you. But I didn't want you to see me looking so bad with a broken arm. You had all those nice-looking men standing around, and I didn't want to be just another one of them. I wanted to meet you when I was looking normal."

"You really did attend that concert? Really?"

"Yes." He told me what I sang and described what I wore.

I could hardly believe his words. Tears filled my eyes. "Oh, God is good."

"That's why I've been asking about God speaking to you. Ullanda, I believe I'm the one for you, and you need to pray about that."

I thought back to the dream. I remembered praying in December when I had demanded an answer from God. "Let's be sure this is God's will," I said. "Let's be open with each other, and give the Lord a chance to work in our lives."

"Yes," he agreed. "That sounds right to me."

After Patrick and I finished talking, he took me home. We talked some more, then we prayed together before he left.

* * *

After Patrick took me home, I thought about the painful and intense praying I'd done that December night. I had cried out for a husband and had asked God to bring him to the concert. God had answered, even though I had not known it then.

That same night other problems had troubled me. I had needed a place to stay, and I did find a room with a Christian friend. I paid no rent and wasn't on the street, but I needed a more permanent place—my own apartment at least. Another problem had been that of transportation. "God, I need a car," I had prayed, "and I can't afford one, so I don't know what to do."

"Lord," I said, "I've made a lot of changes in my life. And I'm still willing to keep on changing. But where I am right now, you know my tastes. I want a Mercedes. You know I don't have any money now, but I want a Mercedes. It doesn't have to be a new one. I'll accept a nice old Mercedes, something from the 1970s is fine. I don't know how You're going to give it to me or how I'm going to pay for it. I don't know what You're going to do."

Three things had been on my heart that night: a husband, a place to live, and a car. I had a place to live, though it was still only temporary. Patrick had come into my life and we already had started to talk about marriage. Was this the beginning of the answers?

I hadn't told Patrick about the dream, even though it seemed clear that he had to be the man I was going to marry. I was scared of making another mistake. I had been hurt those other times, and I wasn't going to go into a wrong relationship again. I had to be totally convinced this was God's will. Those other times—the mistakes I'd made—had seemed like God's will at the time. But I believe I wanted it too much, so I had rushed into things. Now I would wait, and I would be certain.

The next day, Patrick picked me up again for another date. On our way to the restaurant, he said, "Say, you don't have a car, do you? What do you use to get around?"

"I've been praying about it—" I began.

"I'll tell you what, I have a car I'm not using. You can use it if you want to. It's just sitting there on the campus, and I'd planned to sell it, but for some reason I never got around to doing that."

"Really? That would be wonderful." I was too embarrassed to

ask what kind of car. It couldn't be a Mercedes. If it was, he would be driving it instead of the Toyota pickup. Besides, he was a school teacher and couldn't afford a car like that on his salary.

"That's fine," he said. "I'll put it in the shop and have them look it over to make sure it's OK. It's been sitting for about a year and probably needs tuning up at least. When it's ready, I'll bring it out to you."

The same night as we were heading back to where I was staying, I asked, "By the way, what kind of car is it?"

"It's just an old car."

"What year? What kind of car is it?"

"It's just an old Mercedes."

"What year is it?"

"A 1975 model."

Then it hit me! God had answered my prayer. "I can't believe this! I can't believe this!"

"What are you so excited about?"

"That's my prayer. Patrick, before I even met you, I asked the Lord for a husband and a Mercedes—an older model, something in the 1970s."

"No, you didn't ask the Lord for that."

"Yes, I did. In December." Then I told him everything, including the dream about marrying a man whose family spoke French.

"No, I can't believe that," he said. "Why, I've never heard anything like this before."

"I'm telling you the truth." I even told him about Vincent, the man I met at Uchee Pines. "Wow, this is really amazing. Everything is in place now. I know that you are the person."

I held back only one significant fact: that I couldn't have children. I just didn't have the courage to talk about that.

We kept talking and Patrick talked about his own situation. He said his former wife had been a Christian who had turned away from God. Then he started talking about his two children, how much he loved them and missed them. Then he paused and asked the question I dreaded and feared: "Ullanda, do you want to have children?"

Oh, no, I thought, *here it comes.* My heart began to beat faster, and the old feeling of rejection started to surface. And then, a calmness came over me. *If this is the man for me,* I thought, *it won't make any difference.*

"Do you want children?" he asked again.

"Not really. Do you?"

"Why don't you want children?"

"Actually, I can't have children." Then I told him why. I didn't look at him because tears were too near the surface and I didn't want to cry.

"That's fine with me."

"What did you say?"

"I have two children, and don't want any more."

I began to cry in relief. Then I laughed and cried again. "No more doubts, Patrick. You have to be the man for me."

God had answered every part of my prayer except one—a permanent place to live. Yet I knew God would work that out soon. After all, everything else had fallen into place.

Patrick and I started making plans for the wedding and then he said, "Just one thing, Ullanda."

"Yes, what's that?"

"Where you live now is just too far for me to keep coming out to see you. In the best of times, it takes me four hours to make a round trip. That limits the amount of time we can have together. I want to see you—I want to see you every day."

As he talked, I understood the problem. He didn't know that I wanted to get my own apartment.

"Here's an idea," he said. "Since we believe God has planned for us to marry, why don't I start looking for a place for you? A place closer to where I work? When we get married, I'll move in with you. That way we'll already have our own place. I'll pay the rent, and you can live there."

"Come on, you're not serious," I said. "This is too much of a dream come true."

"No, seriously. We'll be all set."

Then I told Patrick the last thing I had asked for. "Just think," I said. "That was December and now it's only February, and God has worked everything out for us." Tears came once again—tears of praise and thanksgiving to God.

Chapter 30

. . . .

CoRine Read ## H3R0 ←

"No way are you going to meet my parents," Patrick exclaimed. Anger seethed through his voice and facial expression.

"But why not?" I was shocked for I'd never seen him behave in such a belligerent way.

"I just don't want you to meet them."

"Patrick, I have to meet your parents," I said.

"Maybe some day in the future. Long after we're married."

"After we get married? Are you crazy? No way is it going to be like that. I'm meeting your parents before the wedding. What's wrong with you?"

"I don't want to invite them to the wedding."

I couldn't believe his attitude and he didn't want to tell me why. Finally he admitted that he and his family had not been on speaking terms since his divorce. His family—especially his father—had insisted, "Once you marry, you don't divorce. You stick with it no matter what happens."

Patrick had protested, "The divorce was not my decision. I didn't want it to end."

"You have two children," his father had said. "Their welfare must come before your desires. You should stay with them, no matter what it takes. You belong with them."

That attitude hurt Patrick deeply. He would have stayed with his former wife if he could have found a way to do so. Patrick, so far as he knew, had tried every way possible to save the marriage. Patrick even set up a counseling appointment with their pastor, hoping this would bring healing. She went with him to one session and refused to go back. Patrick told her he was willing to do anything to save their marriage. They decided on a trial separation, but two months later she served him with divorce papers. He felt devastated and went into depression for a long time.

Patrick had not fought her on anything, because he knew she was determined to end the marriage, no matter what. She asked for and got custody of the children, the house, and all other property except for his 1975 Mercedes and the Toyota pickup.

To add to his personal sadness—especially the loss of his children—his parents' attitude hurt Patrick deeply. He felt they didn't realize his pain, and, in fact, they blamed him for the divorce. In his last conversation with his parents more than a year earlier, Patrick had tried once again to explain, but got nowhere with them. "It doesn't matter what happened," his father insisted. "You need to stay with her because you married her, and she's still your wife in the eyes of God."

At that Patrick declared to his father, "If you're taking her side against your own son, you're not my family anymore. How can you be my parents when you won't believe me or listen to me? So now I've made it complete. I am divorced from my wife, and I'm divorced from my family."

Of course I didn't know any of this until we began to make our wedding plans. After he told me the sad details, I said, "I'm sorry about that, Patrick, but you can't let those things keep you from having a relationship with your family. God isn't pleased with such an attitude. You can't say you're a Christian and hate your family!"

"They turned on me. They took my wife's side and wouldn't listen to me, so I want nothing to do with them."

"That's not right in the eyes of God," I said. "You have to try to work this out. We shouldn't get married until you're in a right relationship with your family. Or at least until you do everything possible to resolve the problems between you."

"They don't want me around," he insisted. "They don't respect me." Slowly, painfully, he told me additional details. The hurt poured out and pain filled my own heart as I listened.

"If you meet them, they might try to destroy our relationship," he added.

"Patrick, I don't care about that. They can't hurt our relationship. But you still have to try. Before we can marry, you have to do everything you can to bring about a reconciliation."

I remained absolutely firm on the matter. Of course, we were praying about it. At last Patrick agreed that he would seek guidance from God on how to bring about a reconciliation. Even to make that much of a concession was terribly hard for him.

A few days later, I went into his dorm room with him. Automatically he flipped on the playback of his answering machine. He had one message. The voice said, "Patrick, this is Judy."

I watched the shock on Patrick's face as he listened to the rest of her message. Judy was his sister.

"Please call me. We miss you and love you, so please call. I've been trying to get in touch with you. I love you, and we want to start talking again."

Patrick flipped off the machine, ignoring my excitement at the message. "It just isn't possible—"

"Of course it's possible," I told him. "At this point, the problem is as much you as it is them. You don't want a relationship with your family." Those words stung, but I had to get through to him.

He fell into a chair and said nothing for a long time. We had prayed for guidance, and I believed this was an answer to prayer. I wasn't going to let him push it aside.

"I don't want anything to do with them," he said slowly. "They turned on me when I was hurting so deeply. The Valcins are my only family now, because they're the only ones who would listen. They cared for me when my own family turned away from me."

"Maybe your family did hurt you and turn away from you," I said, "but you can still reconcile. It's not too late. Judy left that message, didn't she? Can't you hear what your sister is saying to you? They want to make amends. They're trying to apologize. Just ask God to give you the strength to open up."

"I don't want to be rejected again—"

"Rejected? She's begging for reconciliation."

"I can't do it. I can't."

"All right, I'll accept that for now," I said. "But we don't get married until you do reach out. I'm a Christian now, and I'm not getting into a marriage with a family that's not bonded in love. You have to try."

"Ullanda, I love you. I want to marry you, but I don't want them as my family, and I don't want them at my wedding."

We continued to talk, to struggle with the problem. Patrick confessed that Judy had called before and he hadn't returned the calls. The minutes slowly ticked by before he reached for the phone and dialed Judy's number. They talked several minutes and Judy begged him to forgive her and the family.

At last Patrick smiled and the tension left his body. This was the real Patrick, the one I wanted to marry. "And there's something else you need to know," Patrick said, his voice mixed with joy and trepidation. "I've met a wonderful woman. And I'm going to marry her." Judy must have sounded happy for him because he starting telling her about me. Then he held out the phone. "Judy wants to talk to you."

I heard the voice of a sweet woman who told me how much she loved her brother. "Please, Ullanda, help Patrick know that we do love him. I've been talking to my parents. All of us want to get the family together again. We did some cruel things to him. We were shocked and hurt over the news. Instead of helping and comforting Patrick, we turned on him. We thought he was wrong by allowing the divorce. We understand now that his divorce was biblical, that he was the innocent party, and couldn't do anything more to hold their marriage together. Oh, Ullanda, it's a big mess. We want to make things right."

"I'll do what I can," I said. "But I think he's so hurt over his father's attitude—that more than anything else—that he doesn't want to make up with them. If your parents feel as strongly as you say they do, ask them to call him. I'm sure God will help you work through all this."

Patrick and I talked for a long time after we hung up from talking to Judy. I could see his struggle and feel his pain but I could only imagine what he was going through. Sometimes when the pain is buried so deep, it takes time for healing.

Just before he took me home, he said, "All right, I'll pray about reconciling with them."

"That's all I'm asking you to do at this point."

* * *

Time went on. We grew closer, talked about our up-coming marriage, and struggled with Patrick's anger and pain. At last he told me, "If working out things with my parents is the only way you're going to marry me, I agree to contact them. I'll do what I can."

Days passed, but finally Patrick was able to move far enough in resolving his pain to make the first phone call. He spoke to Dada, his Aunt, the one member of the family who had not taken a stand against him. He really loved Dada and felt he could talk to her. He told her he was getting married, that he didn't want his parents to come to the wedding, but I was insisting, and asked her what he should do. "Your future wife is correct," she said. "You have to invite your folks to the wedding, no matter what they've done to you in the past. You have to ask God to give you forgiveness, and put that aside and go on with your life."

He asked Dada to call his parents and talk to them and try to arrange for everybody to get together. She agreed.

Later Patrick told me that Dada called his parents and told them Patrick was getting married, that he wasn't ready to make amends with them, yet he wanted to invite them to the wedding. At first his father responded with, "Doesn't this woman know that he's still married in the eyes of the Lord?" But after Dada explained the situation, Patrick's father realized that he had to leave things in God's care. Most important of all, he loved his son and wanted a reconciliation.

Dada also explained that I was a Christian, that I had a music ministry and often sang with evangelistic meetings, and that I was often featured in the *Breath of Life* crusades. When they heard that, his father said, "Why then this woman must really be converted and this must be of the Lord. We've got to support our son and do whatever we can to work this thing out."

• • •

Patrick's mother called. "Son, we love you and want to get things back together."

At first, he was still cold and stiff.

I listened to one conversation and afterward I said, "You're still holding back in forgiving them."

"I am doing the best I can," Patrick said.

Because I had never gone though anything like this, I couldn't understand how deeply he had been hurt. My family had always stuck by me—even when they didn't agree or didn't like what I did. I knew I would forgive any of them in an instant. To me, his attitude seemed harsh.

Finally I got upset with him and screamed, "You have to forgive them! You're a Christian, and I don't want to marry a man who is acting the way you are."

My words hurt, and I knew it. Then I calmed down. "I'm sorry," I said, "but I thought you were so nice and so loving, yet you can't love your parents. I just don't know how to cope with this."

When he's upset or hurt, Patrick tends to lock it up inside himself and retreat into silence. But this time he got upset and fired back. "You don't understand. They dropped me just when I needed them. I almost lost my life. It got so bad I had to get professional help! My wife filed for divorce and took my children and everything else. When I went to my family for help—just to get them to listen to me and to know they were there for me—they turned their backs on me. They almost destroyed me." Then he quieted and said, "Ullanda, I haven't told you this before but I was so devastated by all this, I wanted to die. I wanted to take my life and thought about suicide. Only, because I'm a Christian, I didn't do that. But I hurt that deeply."

His eyes filled with tears as he tried to choke back the pain he had buried so deeply inside. For 15 years he had tried to be a good husband and father. Then life fell apart. He ended up in a dorm with no money and no other place to live. He had been working hard, taking graduate courses at the university, but he had no one to encourage or comfort him in his pain. "I've been so miserable and alone," he said.

"God can turn it all around," I insisted. "That's why I believe God has put us together."

"Ullanda, I know that, but I can't just push all of this away. Until I met you, I didn't care anymore. I didn't think I could ever be happy—"

"But God brought us together. God will help you—"

"Right now I need time to work through this bitterness."

Finally I understood. Daily I prayed for Patrick to be able to overcome his pain. In the meantime, his parents kept calling, wanting to work things out. I got to speak to them on one occasion and said, "Just be patient with him. He's going through a lot. He wants to come around, and he will."

At last, during one of the phone calls, they reconciled. Patrick had made up his mind to forgive them, but he admitted to me, "I did what was right, but I don't feel it in my heart."

"But you have done all you can do," I said. "God will help you do the rest."

Chapter 32

· ·

No matter how hard I tried, I couldn't get the schedules of our two families coordinated. But Patrick's family did agree to attend the wedding.

One step closer to reconciliation, I kept telling myself.

· · ·

In May of 1991, Yvonne and Valerie Simpson arranged an impressive shower for me at Valerie's house back in New York. Yvonne's cousin, Denise, coordinated everything beautifully. They hired caterers and decorated lavishly. When I walked into Valerie's house and saw so many people who had been part of my life as a jingle singer, I felt ecstatic. Practically everyone I knew in the business had shown up. Everyone brought beautiful gifts, and I felt so happy to be with old friends again.

As I moved around the room, I was able to talk to them individually about my new life and all the miracles that had taken place for me since my conversion. Several of the jingles' singers who weren't Christians listened intently.

"Oh, you made a wonderful decision," one of them said.

Another singer, a Christian, said, "You have really stuck with your faith. I'm proud of you." We talked a little more and she said, "You know, I wish I could let go of these worldly things like you did, and then I could get my life in order."

"Just trust God and ask for help," I said.

"Your life is the best testimony of God at work. You give me the courage to think about making serious changes."

Conversations like that one made my spirits soar. Never had I talked so freely about God and my life before. And most of it came in answer to questions.

I loved every minute of the shower. The most important part for me was that they had invited Patrick's mother and two sisters, all of whom lived in Queens. They came and I got to meet his sisters, Judy and Lisa, as well as his mother, whom they called Mammu. Part Italian with straight black hair and a lovely complexion, Mammu is perhaps two inches over five feet tall and simply beautiful. When we met, I knew she was as sweet as she looked.

After telling them how happy I was to finally meet them, I said. "Now I want to tell you about a dream I had when I went to Uchee Pines." After I shared the dream, I turned to them and said "I dreamed about all of you. I didn't see your faces, but you were speaking French."

They rejoiced with me, thrilled to realize that God had been leading for a long time.

Just before Patrick's family left, I tried again to find a way for our two families to get together. But we couldn't get our times to fit the other's schedule. "So that means we won't be able to meet until the wedding, doesn't it?" I said, feeling quite disappointed.

Then it struck me. "Wait a minute! *The dream.* In the dream our families didn't meet until the day of the wedding!"

"Just unbelievable!" Judy said.

We started to laugh, and we hugged and talked some more. People were snapping pictures all over the place.

That shower was one of the happiest events I had experienced in a long time. God was making life so fantastic and beautiful for me.

● ● ●

Patrick and I decided to get married in Detroit and my family joyfully began to make plans for the wedding. We had hardly gotten past the wedding shower in New York when Aunt Helen called. She was coordinating the wedding. She told me, "Ullanda, you've got to come early and stay here for at least a week."

Our whole family set up our schedule so we could do that.

Verbena flew in and all the members of my family were around for a totally delightful reunion.

When Patrick and I arrived in Detroit, he brought gifts for everybody in the family. Then he said to me, "One thing more I have to do—I must meet your father and ask him for your hand in marriage." He explained that this was the custom he had been brought up to observe and he wanted to do it.

It touched me deeply that he wanted to ask my father. "I'll take you to meet him," I said.

Verbena learned what he was going to do and begged, "Please, would it be OK if I came along and watched when Patrick asks for your hand in marriage?"

"No problem," I said, "except you cry over just about everything. If you start crying in there, you're going to mess up everything."

"I promise I won't cry."

So Patrick, Verbena, and I drove to my dad's apartment. After I introduced them, I saw how nervous my dad was. He knew of our wedding plans, but he had no idea why we had come by. Patrick had bought a little gift for him, a tie clip. This thoughtfulness thrilled Dad.

"Say, what's this?" Patrick noticed a big picture from one of my album covers on my dad's wall. "Is that Ullanda?"

"That's Ullanda, my daughter," Dad said with obvious pride in his voice.

"I've never seen that before." Then he turned from the picture of me made up in jewels, furs, and heavy make-up and said, "Whoa, you were really out there in the world, weren't you?"

"Yes," I said, suddenly realizing that he had heard me talk about my old life, but it hadn't hit him until now.

He gave me a hug. "That's over," he said. "It doesn't matter."

Patrick sat down across from my father. "Mr. McCullough, do you have any questions that you want to ask Ullanda or me? Anything that you'd like to know more about?"

"No, from what I understand you're a nice Christian young man, and that's what I wanted for my daughter, as long as you treat her well."

"You know we're planning to get married, but at the same

time, I was brought up in a traditional home, and we believe in following such customs. So, therefore, I would like to ask you for your daughter's hand in marriage."

Verbena's eyes teared up and then she started to sniffle. I was praying silently, *God, don't let me break down and start crying now.*

My father's eyes widened. He took a deep breath, swallowed, and got a little choked up. "Oh, yes, I definitely consent. You seem to be the perfect person for my daughter, and I'm happy for you. Of course you can have my daughter's hand in marriage."

They both stood and shook hands. Then spontaneously, they embraced each other, then they hugged Verbena and me. What a great moment to see my fiancé come to my dad to ask for my hand in marriage. Even though Mom was dead, I was thankful that my dad was still alive to see all of this take place.

Everybody in my family immediately loved Patrick. They had not liked most of the other men I dated, but they really liked this one. They thought he was a perfect gentleman and very much a Christian.

• • •

Aunt Helen put together the best coed wedding shower I had ever dreamed of. My old high school friends and members from Granddad's church attended. She kept us involved and busy right up until the wedding.

It felt wonderful to have this love and affection from my family and old friends.

• • •

Until the day before our wedding, I still hadn't met Patrick's father or brother, although I had met his mother and sisters at the shower in New York. That evening Aunt Helen had arranged for a big party for both families in what had been my grandparents' home. Because that house held so many good memories for me, I was pleased that Aunt Helen had arranged it there.

Seventeen members of Patrick's family flew into Detroit, including his oldest sister Tanya, his brother Danny with his wife Yolette, as well as his Aunt Evodie and several uncles and nephews. Dada came, and of course, so did his parents. Although he didn't say anything about it, I knew Patrick well enough to realize that their presence touched him deeply. He had been afraid that the family members wouldn't show up. Until he saw them, he wasn't convinced his parents would come. After they promised to come, he had acted as if he had not wanted to see them, but that was a facade. I sensed that, because of his past rejection, he had prepared to face the reality that they would desert him at the last minute. If they hadn't come, his heart would have been truly broken.

Everybody seemed happy, although Patrick remained a little standoffish toward his parents.

Because of the trouble Patrick and his father had, I didn't know how his father would treat me, or whether I would like him. Then we met. No matter what problems had gone on between the two of them, as soon as we were introduced, I knew intuitively that Patrick's father was one of the kindest individuals I'd ever met.

I could see much of Patrick in his father, although they are physically built different. His father is several inches shorter and of a medium build. We had a delightful time that evening. Since they were all Christians, we sang and prayed together, and did a lot of talking. For the first time, I believe Patrick had hope that the reconciliation with his family was going to work.

In the dream, Patrick's father and I were walking together on my wedding day, arm in arm. I assumed that this was what this meant.

• • •

The day of the wedding was beautiful. Everyone was excited, and I was happy that Yvonne could come and be my matron of honor. She and I had been in the world together and gone through so much. Now we were standing together on my wedding day.

Patrick's best friend and his spiritual brother, Gibbs Valcin, was best man. Yvonne's husband, George, and Patrick's sister, Judy, made up the adult portion of the wedding party. Wintley Phipps officiated, he and his family driving in from Washington,

D.C. Because of his heavy schedule, I felt extremely grateful that he would make time to be part of our wedding. His son, Wintson, was the Bible bearer. Seven other children made up the rest of the wedding party.

My former pastor, Clement Murray from New York, also came and assisted in the ceremony. If there was a sad note, it was that none of my friends from the music industry attended. They had given me such a wonderful, loving shower, so I knew they loved me and cared about me. But I still missed them.

We had a large crowd, including church-member friends from New York, as well as people I'd worked with during evangelistic series, such as members of the *Breath of Life*. I also spotted school friends; some of the relationships went back to elementary days. And, of course, all the members of my family were there.

Aunt Helen had planned an outdoor wedding with white chairs set up for the guests. We stood under a huge oak tree, decorated with huge, lovely white bows. In the background, awesome yachts docked on a peaceful river and many of the yacht owners watched from their decks. Perfect weather smiled down on us. On that day, everything was just right, and life could not have been more wonderful.

Wintley Phipps sang with his wonderful baritone voice while I walked down the aisle. I wanted to cry and shout at the same time, as reality hit me. God had finally answered my prayer for a mate to share my life with. *Oh Lord, this is wonderful, and I'm so thankful for what You've done. Especially thank You for giving me this wonderful man You've brought into my life.*

Patrick and I approached from opposite directions and met at the last row of chairs. I took his arm and we walked down the aisle together. A glance told me that Patrick was as near to crying as I was. To me, he looked like Prince Charming, who had come to claim the damsel he had fought for. *This is the beginning of a new life for both of us,* I thought, as we came toward the altar.

A warm glow of praise filled me as I thought of those there with us. My family beamed at me. I smiled at Clement Murray and Wintley Phipps, the two most influential pastors in my life. Yvonne, my best friend and the one person who had been with me through those days of change of direction in my life, was standing at my side. We went through the vows and Pastor Murray read a poignant poem he had written especially for the wedding called, "Tell Her So."

Wintley Phipps sang two songs, the first a love song he had written for his wife and sang at their own wedding. Yvonne sang "The Lord's Prayer."

After Pastor Phipps announced we were husband and wife, Patrick and I kissed each other, then we turned and faced our guests. Next, we planned to approach our parents and family members and pin a small flower on each of them.

As we started toward the family, Pastor Phipps sang the special love song, "Forever Yours." Patrick and I went to his family first. As we moved slowly toward them, I kept thinking, *What is going to happen now? How is Patrick going to react to his father and mother? What will he do? Is he going to shake their hands? Ignore them?* I held my breath and felt myself tighten inside, afraid that this would be an awkward scene.

Patrick paused in front of his father. The two men stared into each others' eyes for what seemed like a long time, but it was probably only two or three seconds. Then a sob came from Patrick, as he reached out and hugged his father. His father cried too. I didn't look around, but I could hear crying all around us. "Oh God, thank you, thank you," I whispered again and again. I had hoped for a demonstration of reconciliation, but I hadn't expected it to be so overwhelming.

Then I started to cry.

Patrick was crying.

Both his parents were crying.

As far as I could tell, every member of his family was weeping and hugging each other.

After we went through his whole family we went to mine, embracing each in turn. Aunt Helen broke down and wept as if her heart were breaking. Since my mother's death, she had been a mother to me, and I think she felt it keenly at that moment as if she were saying goodbye to her own daughter. She cried and held tightly and wouldn't let go of me. I must have stood there with her for a full minute. All the while, Pastor Phipps continued to sing "Forever Yours."

Just then Yvonne embraced me, and I let go of all my heaviness and concern that had been stored up inside. The fears and pain flowed out of me and a deep-felt joy and peace filled my heart. Then the harpist played as the recessional began. Patrick and I paused long enough to smile at each other. He clasped my hand. In that moment, both of us felt that invisible bonding that made us one with each other and with God.

Our wedding took place on July 14, 1991.

We were now husband and wife.

We were now ready for our life together.

And it would be a great life with God leading both of us.

I Read it & decided Its a

Wonderful story, So please

chill out, relax, slow down, &

prop up your legs & read

O.K. always come trust Jesus

always. O.K Sorry about the pen

changes, my wife I love you World

without end. Peace & Grace in christ

Jesus!.

Epilogue

· ·

An important person came into my life in October of 1991. Because of her impact, this book wouldn't be complete without acknowledging her. I had flown to Virginia to sing at a conference called "Youth to Youth." Its theme was "Say No to Drugs." Afterward quite a number of people crowded around me, buying tapes and just as often simply talking to me about my ministry. Beyond the crowd, I saw an attractive woman standing apart from the others. People kept talking, and I assumed she would get tired of waiting and go on. But she remained.

After a good five minutes of mainly listening to one man, I interrupted him to say to the woman, "I'll be with you in a moment."

"No problem, take your time, finish with them first." She had such a warm smile that I felt attracted to her. Finally the others moved on and we were able to talk.

"My name is Esther Sanidad." She spoke with the slightest accent. Her face shone with genuine joy. As I later found out, she had been born in the Philippines, was married to a doctor, and lived in Ohio. She brought several youth to the rally in her van.

Our conversation flowed so easily, even though we'd never met before. I was drawn to her warmth and sincerity.

Just before she left she said, "My pastor wants me to ask if you would be willing to come to Ohio and do a concert for our church."

"Sure, I'd love to do that. Just let me know when."

We talked another few minutes, and she took my card. "I'll call you," she told me as we parted.

I hoped she'd call for I wanted to know her better.

During that time, I had been praying for God to send me a person who could book concerts, do some promotion, and send out packets of information. Because so much of my work required my being out of town, it was hard to respond to requests and keep up to date on everything.

A couple of weeks later Esther phoned me in California, and we set up a concert at her home church in Marion, Ohio. During our conversation, she asked, "Who does your booking?"

"No one," I said with a laugh. "In fact, I need assistance in that area."

A slight pause followed before she said, "Let's pray about it first, but I'd like to work with you."

"Really? You're really interested in helping me?" As I was getting over the surprise I realized that she wanted to offer her services as a form of ministry. Certainly she wasn't trying to make money, but she needed to be sure that this was what God wanted her to do.

A few days later, Esther phoned me. "Yes," she said, "I've prayed about it, and I would definitely like to help you."

"Wow! Let's go for it!"

"I'll help you by taking care of your business, then you can devote your time to singing and doing the ministry God has given you to do."

Esther didn't know it then, but she was an answer to prayer. She has remained my right arm and a dear friend.

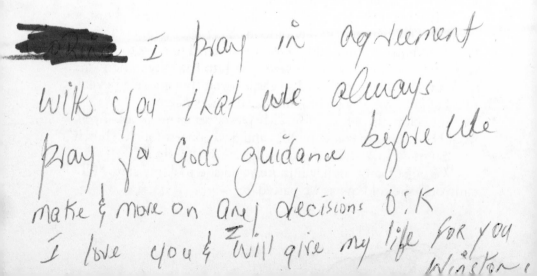

~~Celine~~ I pray in agreement with you that we always pray for Gods guidance before we make & more on any decisions O.K I love you & will give my life for you
Winston